Why Is My Choice of a Bible Translation So Important?

Bible Versions and Abbreviations Mentioned in this Booklet:

CEV: Contemporary English Version (1995)
ESV: English Standard Version (2001)
GNB: Good News Bible: Today's English Version Second Edition (1992)
HCSB: Holman Christian Standard Bible (2003)
KJV: King James Version (1611)
LB: *The Living Bible—Paraphrased* (1971)
Message: *The Message* (1995)
NASB: New American Standard Bible (1963, 1995)
NCV: New Century Version (1987, 1991)
NET: The New English Translation (2001)
NIV: New International Version (1984)
NKJV: New King James Version (1982)
NLT: New Living Translation (1996)
NRSV: New Revised Standard Version (1989)
Phillips: The New Testament in Modern English by J. B. Phillips (1960)
REB: Revised English Bible (1989)
RSV: Revised Standard Version (1946, 1952, 1971)
SB: *The Word on the Street* (formerly titled *The Street Bible*) (2003)
TNIV: Today's New International Version (2005)

Why Is My Choice of a Bible Translation So Important?

By Wayne Grudem
with Jerry Thacker

Choosing which Bible to read and trust is an
important decision. Christians need to care enough about
their own sanctification to choose a translation that
conveys the very words of God.

Why Is My Choice of a Bible Translation So Important?

Published by
The Council on Biblical Manhood and Womanhood
2825 Lexington Road, Box 926
Louisville, KY 40280

The Council on Biblical Manhood and Womanhood was established in 1987 for the purpose of studying and setting forth Biblical teachings on the relationship between men and women, especially in the home and church.

Cover design: Bowin Tichenor

First printing, October 2005

Printed in the United States of America

ISBN: 0-9773968-0-0

Contents

Foreword

In 2002 Zondervan and the International Bible Society (IBS) announced plans to publish a revision of the New International Version (NIV) known as Today's New International Version (TNIV). At that time they released only the New Testament. In response to this, The Council on Biblical Manhood and Womanhood (CBMW) and many evangelical leaders expressed their concerns, particularly over the gender-neutralization of hundreds of passages.

Since then, much discussion has taken place through debates, radio programs, and writing. Now, in 2005, Zondervan and IBS published the full TNIV including both the Old and New Testaments, in spite of broad and deep evangelical resistance. This highlighted, once again, the need for the Christian community to be informed about the differences between various Bible translations.

This booklet, then, is the product of CBMW's thorough review of the entire TNIV. It is offered to those who want a brief overview of the concerns regarding gender-neutral Bible translations, with the hope that we will all gain a greater appreciation for God's Word and be better informed as we make decisions about which translation we use.

The material in the appendices was prepared under the general oversight of CBMW. Special thanks goes to Brian Reed, Gary Steward, Tracy McKenzie, Wayne Jenks, Jason Glas, Vern Poythress, Travis Buchanan, Steve Eriksson, Robert Polen, and Trent Poling. I would like to thank Tim Dick and Ligonier Ministries as well for their generosity in developing this resource. Also special thanks to Heather Tjader for her work in the layout and editing of this booklet.

It is our desire at CBMW that you have information that will help you dig deeper in your own analysis of various Bible translations. We will continue to pray for all involved in this debate.

Randy Stinson
Executive Director
The Council on Biblical Manhood and Womanhood~October 2005

Key Issues Regarding Bible Translation

A Little History

If you went into a Christian bookstore back in the 1960's, you could usually count on the fingers of just one hand the number of Bible translations on the shelves. Most people knew that there were two broad categories of the types of Bibles you would find. Some followed a "word-for-word" or "essentially literal" translation philosophy. An *essentially literal* translation "strives to translate the exact words of the original-language text in a translation, but not in such a rigid way as to violate the normal rules of language and syntax" of the translation language.[1]

The other category of Bibles was based on a "dynamic equivalence" or "thought-for-thought" translation philosophy. A *dynamic equivalence* translation seeks to reproduce the thoughts or ideas of the original text in the way a modern speaker would say them. Thus, whenever something in the original-language text is foreign or unclear to a contemporary reader, the original text should be translated in terms of a "dynamic equivalent"—a meaning in the

---

[1] Leland Ryken, *The Word of God in English: Criteria for Excellence in Bible Translation* (Wheaton: Crossway, 2002), 19. Sometimes essentially literal translations are also called "word for word" translations.

translation language that corresponds to or is "equivalent" to a meaning in the original-language text.[2]

A good illustration of the difference between essentially literal and dynamic equivalence translations is found in 1 Kings 2:10, which says, in the King James Version, "So David slept with his fathers and was buried in the city of David." This wording is followed by most essentially literal translations because that is literally what the Hebrew text says (using Hebrew words for "slept" and "with" and "fathers").

But dynamic equivalence translators would object that people today don't say someone "slept with his fathers" – they just say that he "died." So the New Living Translation (NLT), for example, says, "Then David died and was buried in the city of David." The translation is a "thought-for-thought" translation because the main thought or idea – the idea that David died and was buried — *is expressed in a way that modern speakers would use to express the same idea today.*

However, not everyone thinks that is an improvement. Supporters of essentially literal translations object that some details are missing in the translation "then David died." This dynamic equivalence translation does not include the idea of sleeping as a rich metaphor for death, a metaphor in which there is a veiled hint of some day awakening from that sleep to a new life. So a hint of future

---

[2] Ibid., 18.

resurrection is missing. The expression "slept with his fathers" also includes a hint of a corporate relationship with David's ancestors who had previously died, but this is also missing from the dynamic equivalence translation, "then David died."

Supporters of essentially literal translations would agree that the dynamic equivalence rendering "then David died" does translate the *main idea* into contemporary English, but they would add that it is better to translate *all of the words* of the Hebrew original, including the word *shakab* (which means, "to lie down, sleep"), and the words *'im* (which means "with"), and *'ab* (which means "father," and in the plural, "fathers"), since these words are in the Hebrew text as well. When these words are translated, not just the main idea but also *more details of the meaning* of the Hebrew original are brought over into English.

In response, supporters of dynamic equivalence translations say that modern readers won't easily understand the literal translation, "David slept with his fathers." But essentially literal supporters reply that they will understand, because the rest of the sentence says that David was buried: "Then David slept with his fathers *and was buried* in the city of David" (1 Kings 2:10, ESV). The larger context begins in v. 1, "When David's time to die drew near..." (1 Kings 2:1). Modern readers may have to ponder the expression for a moment, but then they will understand it and will then have access to much greater richness of meaning that was there in the original text.

Today, there are three categories of Bible translations. They include:

Essentially Literal: These include the English Standard Version (ESV), New American Standard Bible (NASB), Holman Christian Standard Version (HCSB), New King James Version (NKJV), King James Version (KJV), Revised Standard Version (RSV), New Revised Standard Version (NRSV), and the *NET Bible*.

Dynamic Equivalence: These include the New Living Translation (NLT), the Contemporary English Version (CEV), the New Century Version (NCV), the Revised English Bible (REB), and the Good News Bible (GNB).

Paraphrase: These include The Message (Message), The Living Bible (LB), The New Testament in Modern English (Phillips), and The Word on the Street (previously called The Street Bible) (SB). These translations are even freer than dynamic equivalence translations in how they render Biblical passages, often finding creative new ways to express the general idea of a verse.

Mixed versions: Two popular translations do not fall exactly into the previous categories. The New International Version (NIV) and Today's New International Version (TNIV) contain substantial elements of dynamic equivalence translation mixed with a basic commitment to essentially literal translation, so they are a mixture of the two types.

Gender-Neutral Bible Translations

In recent years, a new controversy has arisen over "gender-neutral Bibles." Called "gender accurate" or "gender inclusive" by their advocates, these translations change thousands of verses by removing the male-oriented words "father," "son," "brother," "man," and "he/him/his" from places where these words were good, accurate translations of the original Greek or Hebrew. In such places these gender-neutral Bibles only translate the *general idea* of the passage and *omit male-oriented details of meaning.* Thus, while the changes may sound more acceptable in our contemporary context, details of meaning in the original text are lost.

Several translations that employ extensive gender-neutral language include the following: NRSV, TNIV, NLT, NCV, GNB, and CEV. The translations that have adopted gender-neutral Bible language most often are those that follow a dynamic equivalence theory, although this is not necessarily the case. The Living Bible is a dynamic equivalence version that accurately renders gender language. But the New Revised Standard Version is an essentially literal translation that systematically adopts gender-neutral language.

Thus, adopting gender-neutral language is not necessary for a dynamic equivalence version, since it is no harder to say, "If your brother sins," than it is to say, "If your brother or sister sins." It is no harder to say, "son of man," than "mere mortals." It is no harder to say, "Blessed is the man" than it is to say, "Blessed are those." The most important difference is not over theories of translation but rather about whether to convey in English the gender-specific ideas of the original text.

Are you reading the very words of the living God?

The really important question every man and woman must ask when it comes to the Bible translation they choose is very simple: "Are these the very words of God?" You want to have confidence in the fact that God's words to you in your own Bible are, as much as is humanly possible, translating *exactly* what was recorded in the original languages by the original authors. There are several good reasons for desiring this and expecting this from a translation.

1. Every word of God is important.

First, notice how the Bible itself places an incredibly high value on the importance of every word that God has spoken to us:

2 Timothy 3:16 – "*All Scripture* is breathed out by God and profitable for teaching, for reproof, for correction, and for training in righteousness." [3]

2 Peter 1:20-21 – "knowing this first of all, that no prophecy of Scripture comes from someone's own interpretation. For no prophecy was ever produced by the will of man, but men spoke from God as they were *carried along by the Holy Spirit.*"

Proverbs 30:5 – "*Every word* of God proves true; he is a shield to those who take refuge in him."

Psalm 12:6 – "The words of the LORD are *pure words*, like silver refined in a furnace on the ground, purified seven times."

Matthew 4:4 – "But he answered, 'It is written, "Man shall not live by bread alone, but by *every word* that comes from

---

[3] All Scripture quotations are taken from the English Standard Version (ESV), unless otherwise noted.

the mouth of God.'""''

Revelation 22:18 – "I warn everyone who hears the *words* of the prophecy of this book: if anyone adds to them, God will add to him the plagues described in this book."

2. God's words have more depth of meaning than anybody knows.

It is remarkable to see how Jesus and the New Testament authors can make arguments that depend on the smallest details of the Bible's words. For example, sometimes they make arguments that depend on a single word or even a single letter of Old Testament Scripture. Note the following examples:

In Matthew 22:42-45, Jesus asked a question of the religious leaders:

> "What do you think about the Christ? Whose son is he?" They said to him, "The son of David." He said to them, "How is it then that David, in the Spirit, calls him Lord, saying, "'The Lord said *to my Lord*, Sit at my right hand, until I put your enemies under your feet'? [a quotation from Psalm 110:1] If then David calls him Lord, how is he his son?"

The word "my" in "my Lord" comes from a single letter of the Hebrew alphabet (the letter *yod*). Jesus makes an argument based on a single letter of the Old Testament text! It is all God's words, and it is all trustworthy.

Matthew 5:18 – For truly, I say to you, until heaven and earth pass away, not an iota, not a dot, will pass from the Law until all is accomplished.

In the Greek language, *"iota"* was the name of the Hebrew *yod*, the smallest letter of the Hebrew alphabet. And the word translated "dot" represented a small point or projection on an individual letter of the Hebrew alphabet. Jesus is saying that *every detail* of meaning in God's Word will be fulfilled.

Galatians 3:16: Now the promises were made to Abraham and to his offspring. It does not say, "And to offsprings," referring to many, but referring to one, "And to your offspring," who is Christ.

Paul argues on the basis of the fact that a noun is singular and not plural in the Old Testament texts of Genesis 13:15; 17:7.

Jesus and Paul were willing to depend on the tiniest details of God's words in the Old Testament. They knew that God had planned his Word in such a way that it would give sufficient guidance for all of his people throughout all cultures and societies for all time. His Word is the product of his infinite wisdom and all the details of meaning are there for a purpose, and often for multiple purposes, that only God knew and understood. The connections between words, phrases, sentences, and paragraphs, and the relationships between the various parts of Scripture, are more complex than any one human being will ever understand.

Therefore if a particular translation philosophy results in translators omitting or adding details to the text of Scripture, even if the translators act from good motives, they change the meaning and the application of the text in ways that they may not intend or even realize. That is why God warns against changing his Word. *Therefore in translating we should not change God's words for something else or change the meaning of God's words.*

3. All Christians need to make sound decisions about the Bibles they buy and use.

Sometimes supporters of gender-neutral Bibles claim that the controversy is just an obscure argument between scholars about their favorite translation theory. This implies that lay persons should not get involved in the controversy but should just trust scholars in their judgments. This is a misleading way to represent the controversy.

Let's look at the principles involved. We'll use Today's New International Version (TNIV) as our example. Underneath all of the pages of argument about the TNIV there is a basic, very simple question: *Should Bible translations avoid using specific male examples to teach a broader truth?*

For example, should we avoid using male-oriented words to translate Psalm 1:1, "Blessed is the man who does not walk in the counsel of the wicked"? Is the word "man" offensive or objectionable, even when the original Hebrew text clearly means "the man" and refers to an example of an individual male person? Should we avoid using male-oriented words to translate Luke 17:3, "If your brother sins, rebuke him, and if he repents, forgive him," even when the original Greek text clearly means "your brother" and "him"? Should we avoid using male-oriented words to translate Proverbs 13:1, "A wise son heeds his father's instruction," even when the original Hebrew clearly means "son" (not "child") and "father" (not "parent")?

In the TNIV, in over 3,600 examples like these the question is not really the meaning of a Greek or Hebrew word (for those meanings of ancient words have not changed). Nor is it a question of technical translation theory that lay persons cannot understand.

The question is, *when there is a male-specific example in the original Greek or Hebrew text, should we translate it as a male-*

specific example in English? The TNIV translators have decided, "No, we should not, but should make the translation more gender-neutral." But those who object to the TNIV say, "Yes, we should keep the male-specific example that is there in the original language. We should translate the meaning of the original text as accurately as we can in English."

4. Gender-neutral Bibles (like the TNIV and NLT) change thousands of singular verses to plural and thus diminish the Bible's emphasis on individual responsibility and relationship with God.

Once again, let's use the newest gender-neutral Bible, the TNIV, as an example. When the TNIV changes James 1:12 from "Blessed is <u>the man</u> who perseveres under trial, because when <u>he</u> has stood the test, <u>he</u> will receive the crown of life" to "Blessed are <u>those</u> who persevere under trial, because when <u>they</u> have stood the test, <u>they</u> will receive the crown of life," we are suddenly talking about *a group* that perseveres and *a group* that receives a reward. The emphasis on *an individual* persevering under trial is lost. Someone might wonder, "What if I persevere under trial but others in my group do not? Will I still receive a reward or not? And will this be a group reward (like the Super Bowl trophy), since it says '*they* will receive the crown of life'?

Make that kind of change over 2,000 times (as the TNIV has done) and you have changed a major focus of the entire Bible. The Bible has much emphasis on individual responsibility before God and an individual person's relationship to God, but that is greatly watered down by thousands of inaccurate plurals in the TNIV Bible. This is a serious alteration of the Word of God.

In addition to these more than 2000 changes of singulars to plurals, the TNIV makes over 1600 more changes of other kinds to remove men and male-oriented words from the Bible, sometimes just deleting words completely, sometimes by doing things like changing "son" to "children" and "father" to "parent."

But were the problems fixed in the 2005 edition? After the TNIV New Testament received so much criticism in 2002, some people heard a rumor that they "fixed the problems" in the 2005 TNIV, which includes both the New Testament and the Old Testament. In fact, while they changed a handful of verses for the better, they changed others for the worse. The research scholars working with The Council on Biblical Manhood and Womanhood in Louisville, Kentucky went through the entire 2005 edition of the TNIV and updated their online list of translation inaccuracies in the TNIV (www.no-tniv.com). For the New Testament that list has now been changed from

901 inaccuracies for the 2002 New Testament to 910 inaccuracies for the 2005 New Testament. And another 2,776 inaccuracies have now been added for the Old Testament, making a total of 3,686 translation inaccuracies in the TNIV (see the entire list at the end of this booklet, or see www.no-tniv.com or www.cbmw.org). No, the problems have not at all been fixed! The same gender-neutral policies prevail.

5. The real controversy is whether to water down or omit details of meaning that modern culture finds offensive.

The deepest difference over gender-neutral translations is not really about whether people will be able to understand the Bible today. Rather, it is about whether translators should exclude details that seem culturally offensive in the contemporary culture.

After all, the words in dispute are only five: "father," "son," "brother," "man," and "he/him/his." *What young person 18-34 cannot understand these words?* The ultimate reason for deleting these words thousands of times is not that people cannot understand them, for they are extraordinarily simple and common words. The ultimate reason is that the translators decided it was objectionable today to translate literally the Bible's uses of an individual male example to teach a general truth in thousands of passages.

For example, it is not that young adults cannot understand, "Blessed is the man who does not walk in the counsel of the wicked" (Psalm 1:1). It is that the gender-neutral Bible translators find it objectionable that the Bible used a single male example to teach a general truth, so they changed the meaning to "Blessed are *those* ... ". It is not that young adults cannot understand the words, "If your *brother* sins, rebuke him, and if he repents, forgive him" (Luke 17:3). Nor would young adults have any difficulty in realizing that the verse also *applies* to a sister who sins, any more than they would have difficulty understanding that "you shall not covet your neighbor's *wife*" (Exodus 20:17) also *applies* to not coveting your neighbor's husband!

For centuries people have easily understood that when the Bible uses an example of an individual man or woman to teach a general principle, the principle also applies to people of the opposite sex. The parable of the persistent widow (Luke 18:1-8) teaches both men and women about persistence in prayer. The parable of the prodigal son (Luke 15:11-32) also applies to prodigal daughters.[4] We do not have to change the words of the Bible for such general applications to be understood. The Bible frequently

---

[4] The TNIV does not change these parables to anything gender-neutral.

teaches by using concrete, specific examples, not just vague principles and not just groups.

So the controversy is not really about whether young people can understand that "If your brother sins, rebuke him" also *applies* to a sister who sins. Rather, the problem is that the TNIV translators found it objectionable that Jesus used an individual example of a male human being ("If your brother sins...") to teach a general truth. Therefore the TNIV changed Jesus' words to "If a brother or sister sins against you ...," adding "or sister" and "against you," which are words that Jesus did not say), and in doing so they failed to translate Jesus' words accurately.

The bottom line issue, then, is not whether the Bible should be understandable today. Nobody is arguing for the preservation of archaic words like "thee" or "thou." The bottom line issue is that gender-neutral translations such as the TNIV omit details of meaning in many hundreds of verses because of the translator's objections to the male-specific meaning of those verses. They found the Bible's frequent use of male-specific examples to be offensive in the modern culture, and they decided not to translate them accurately as a result.

6. The Deepest Danger

The deepest danger in adopting gender-neutral policies such as those by which the TNIV was translated is that hundreds of other details that the modern culture finds offensive may be watered down in future translations. More and more, we will have a Bible that does not accurately represent in English what the original Hebrew and Greek languages said. Rather these Bibles will represent something that the translators think will be a little more acceptable in modern culture. But then we no longer have the Word of God in all its wisdom and richness. Instead, we have the Word of God mixed with the words of man.

7. Be careful which Bible you recommend and which one you choose.

Choosing which Bible to read and trust is an important decision. Christians need to care enough about their own sanctification to choose a translation that conveys the very words of God. Look for a Bible that you can use and trust as your daily study Bible. Remember, something that has thousands of "words of man" that are not accurately representing the very words of God will have a harmful effect on your Christian life, your walk with God, and your church. May God help you to choose wisely.

Appendix 1: Some Examples of Changed Verses in The TNIV

Here are eight examples of verses changed by the TNIV, with a short comment about the change in meaning in each case. When you realize that the TNIV has over 3,600 changes like this, you can see that the TNIV's policy on gender language has made it to be a significantly different Bible from the NIV. Can it really be trusted as the very words of God?

Psalm 8:4

NIV: What is <u>man</u> that you are mindful of him, the <u>son of man</u> that you care for him?

TNIV: What are <u>mere mortals</u> that you are mindful of them, <u>human beings</u> that you care for them?

Change in meaning: The singular "man" meaning "the human race" is changed to plural "mere mortals," wrongly removing the sense of unity of the human race (the Hebrew is singular). The word "mortals" also places an incorrect emphasis on mortality (or being subject to death), which the Hebrew word does not mean, and which is not part of the essence of man as created by God.

The Hebrew singular *ben* which means "son" and the singular *'adam* which means "man" are incorrectly translated with the plural "human beings," removing masculine meaning, and thus removing the title "son of man," which Jesus often used of himself. (The TNIV also incorrectly removes "son of man" when this verse is quoted in Hebrew 2:6.)

Psalm 34:20

NIV: He protects all <u>his</u> bones, not one of them will be broken.

TNIV: He protects all <u>their</u> bones, not one of them will be broken.

Change in meaning: The 3rd person masculine singular "his" rightly represents the 3rd person masculine singular pronoun suffix in Hebrew, but the TNIV incorrectly pluralizes this to "their bones." This obscures the fulfillment of this verse in Christ's crucifixion in John 19:36, which says, "For these things took place that the Scripture might be fulfilled: "Not one of his bones will be broken."

This part of Psalm 34 speaks of God's protection of an individual righteous man: God protects "his bones." Why does the TNIV refuse to translate hundreds of 3rd person masculine singular pronouns in the original languages as 3rd person masculine singular pronouns in English? What is the objection to male-oriented language when it accurately reflects the original Hebrew or Greek text?

Matthew 7:4

NIV: How can you <u>say to your brother</u>, 'Let me take the speck out of your eye,' when all the time there is a plank in your own eye?

TNIV: How can you <u>say</u>, 'Let me take the speck out of your eye,' when all the time there is a plank in your own eye?

Change in meaning: The entire phrase "to your brother" is left out. But Jesus said these words (Greek *to adelpho sou*). Are we free to just take masculine words out of the Bible?

John 14:23

NIV: If <u>anyone</u> loves me, <u>he</u> will obey my teaching. My Father will love <u>him</u>, and we will come to <u>him</u> and make our home with <u>him</u>.

TNIV: <u>Anyone</u> who loves me will obey my teaching. My Father will love <u>them</u>, and we will come to <u>them</u> and make our home with <u>them</u>.

Change in meaning: The "If" that Jesus said (Greek *ean*) is omitted, and three masculine singular pronouns (Greek *autos*) are incorrectly translated with "them," removing the amazing emphasis on the Father and Son dwelling with an individual person. In the TNIV, maybe "them" refers the whole group of those who obey. How can we know?

This verse also illustrates another serious result of systematically changing singulars to plurals in thousands of cases: The TNIV will ultimately lead to a loss of confidence in *tens of thousands* of plural pronouns in the Bible. Preachers and Bible teachers cannot rightly use the TNIV to make a point based on the plurals "they/them/their/those" or the second person pronouns "you/your/yours" because they can no longer have confidence that those represent accurately the meaning of the original. Maybe the original was plural ("their") but then again maybe "their" is a gender-neutral substitute for a singular ("his"). Maybe the original was 2nd person ("you") but then again maybe "you" is a gender-neutral substitute for a 3rd person singular pronoun ("he") or a singular noun ("a man").

How can ordinary English readers know? They can't. So no weight can be put on those pronouns. "He" in the NIV has become "we" or "you" or "they" in the TNIV thousands of times.

How many pronouns are thrown into doubt? The forms of "we/us/our/ourselves" occur 4,636 times, of "you/your/yours/yourselves" 21,205 times, and the forms of "they/them/their/themselves/those" 19,372 times, for a total of 45,213 pronouns. How can we know which of these 45,213 are trustworthy, and which are the TNIV's gender-neutral substitutes for the correct translation "he/him/his"? The only way is to check the Hebrew and Greek text in each case, and who is going to do that? Can you really study, or memorize, or teach or preach from such a Bible where you can't trust this many pronouns?

1 Corinthians 15:21
NIV: For since death came through a <u>man</u>, the resurrection of the dead comes also through a <u>man</u>.

TNIV: For since death came through a <u>human being</u>, the resurrection of the dead comes also through a <u>human being</u>.

Change in meaning: Here the Greek word is *anthropos*, which can mean either "man" or "person," depending on context. But in this context it refers to Adam and Christ and the meaning "man" is appropriate. What is the objection to calling Adam a "man"? What is the objection to calling Jesus a "man"? This verse also shows that people are wrong when they claim that "the TNIV didn't change any masculine language referring to God or Christ." Here it did (and it did so in the next example as well).

The TNIV web site says that inclusive-language Bibles like the TNIV "introduce inclusive language only with reference to human beings and only when the original author intended to include both sexes. (www.tniv.info, under "The TNIV and Gender Accurate Language" by Mark Strauss, Ph.D., Member of the NIV's Committee on Bible Translation, accessed Sept. 22, 2005). But here it introduces inclusive language, so does this mean we are to think of Adam and Christ as being of "both sexes," both men and women? Why does the TNIV use inclusive language to refer to Adam and Christ?

Hebrews 2:17

NIV: For this reason he had to be made like his <u>brothers</u> in every way, in order that he might become a merciful and faithful high priest in service to God, and that he might make atonement for the sins of the people.

TNIV: For this reason he had to be made like his <u>brothers and sisters</u> in every way, in order that he might become a merciful and faithful high priest in service to God, and that he might make atonement for the sins of the people.

Change in meaning: Did Jesus have to become like his sisters "in every way" in order to become a "high priest in service to God"? All the OT priests were men, and surely the high priest was only a man. This text does not quite proclaim an androgynous Jesus (who was both male and female), but it surely leaves open a wide door for misunderstanding, and almost invites misunderstanding. Meditate on that phrase "in every way" and see if you can trust the TNIV.

Revelation 3:20

NIV: I stand at the door and knock. If anyone hears my voice and opens the door, I will come in and eat with <u>him</u>, and <u>he</u> with me.

TNIV: I stand at the door and knock. If anyone hears my voice and opens the door, I will come in and eat with <u>them</u>, and <u>they</u> with me.

Change in meaning: The idea of Christ coming into an individual person's life is lost; Christ no longer eats with "him" but with "them." Readers may well understand "them" to refer to the plural group "those whom I love" in the previous verse, so the TNIV now pictures Christ coming into a church and eating among a group of people. The clear teaching on individual fellowship with Christ is blurred.

Revelation 22:18

NIV: I warn everyone who hears the words of the prophecy of this book: If <u>anyone</u> adds anything to them, God will add to <u>him</u> the plagues described in this book.

TNIV: I warn everyone who hears the words of the prophecy of this scroll: If <u>any one of you</u> adds anything to them, God will add to <u>you</u> the plagues described in this scroll.

Change in meaning: The first "you" added by the TNIV is plural, referring to the whole group of hearers. Therefore the second "you" is also plural, and if anyone in the group adds to the words of prophecy the penalty is now expanded from the one person ("him") to the whole group. This is a change in meaning in the very verse that warns against changing the words of this prophecy!

Appendix 2: A Complete List of 3,686 Inaccurate Translations in the TNIV

We have included here a list of 3,686 translation inaccuracies in the TNIV which you can check for yourself (2,776 in the Old Testament and 910 in the New Testament). There is also a chart at the end with a summary of inaccuracies by category.

Gender-Related Translation Inaccuracies in the 2005 TNIV Old Testament: A Categorized List of 2,776 Examples

Note: This list of translation inaccuracies has been based on the 2005 edition of *Today's New International Version*, in comparison with the 1984 edition of the New International Version. The changes here involve the removal of five words: "father," "brother," "man," "son," and "he/him/his."

In every case listed, the 1984 NIV had translated the gender-related term accurately, but it was removed and replaced with an inaccurate gender-neutral word or phrase in the 2005 TNIV. It seems to us that every example in this list eliminates masculine meaning or nuance that is present in the original Hebrew text, and also that the changes frequently go beyond the legitimate bounds of ordinary, well-established meanings for the common Hebrew words being translated. These 2,776 examples therefore seem to us to be "translation inaccuracies" that were included in the TNIV for the sake of producing a more "gender neutral" or "inclusive language" version of the Bible. Such re-wording may seem more acceptable in today's secular culture, but it is not a more accurate way of translating the Word of God. There is a wrongful removal of male-oriented meaning in over 2,700 places in the Old Testament. (See below for a similar list of 910 inaccuracies in the TNIV New Testament.)

A complete tally of the number of errors by category is found at the end of this list.

This list was prepared under the general oversight of The Council on Biblical Manhood and Womanhood, and has been compared for accuracy against the Hebrew Old Testament. In the event that readers may find any corrections or additions that should be made to this list, we would welcome your input sent to: office@cbmw.org.

A. Changes Made from Singular to Plural (and a Few Related Changes) to Avoid the Use of "He/Him/His"

1. Changing 3rd person singular "he/him/his/himself" to 3rd person plural ("they/them/their/themselves") (857 inaccuracies)

Comment: There is no question that the Hebrew pronouns and verbs in these verses are singular. The Hebrew text of the Old Testament has not changed. But the TNIV has translated over 2,000 singulars as plurals, just to avoid using the offensive words "he/him/his." (Categories 1-6 and category 19 on this list all show changes from singulars to plurals). The result is a significant reduction in the Bible's emphasis on individual relationship with God and individual responsibility before God.

Examples:

Psalm 1:3
NIV: <u>He</u> is like a tree planted by streams of water, which yields its fruit in season and whose leaf does not wither. Whatever <u>he</u> does prospers.

TNIV: <u>They</u> are like a tree planted by streams of water, which yields its fruit in season and whose leaf does not wither—whatever <u>they</u> do prospers.

Jeremiah 31:34
NIV: No longer will <u>a man</u> ('ish) teach <u>his</u> neighbor, or a man his brother, saying, 'Know the LORD,' because they will all know me, from the least of them to the greatest," declares the LORD.

TNIV: No longer will <u>they</u> teach <u>their</u> neighbors, or say to one another, 'Know the LORD,' because they will all know me, from the least of them to the greatest," declares the LORD.

Complete List:
Gen. 1:27, 5:1, 6:3 (x2), 9:6; **Exod.** 13:14, 21:15, 21:21 (x2), 25:2; **Lev.** 17:4 (x2), 17:9, 19:8, 19:13, 19:33, 19:34, 24:15, 25:13, 25:15, 25:26 (x2), 25:27 (5x), 25:28 (x3), 27:10 (x2), 27:29; **Num.** 5:10, 9:13, 11:10, 12:6 (x2), 15:31, 19:19 (3x), 19:20, 24:20, 32:18; **Deut.** 10:18, 13:8 (x4), 13:9 (x2), 13:10 (x2), 14:21, 15:2 (x3), 15:8 (x2), 15:12 (x2), 28:44

(x3), 29:19, 29:20 (x3), 29:21; **Josh.** 2:19 (x4); **1 Kgs.** 8:42; **1 Chron.** 16:43; **Ezra** 1:3 (x3), 1:4, 2:1, 6:11 (x3, Aramaic); **Neh.** 5:13, 11:3, 11:20; **Esther** 4:11 (x2); **Job** 3:19, 4:17, 7:1, 7:10 (x4), 7:17 (x2), 7:18 (x2), 8:14 (x2), 8:15 (x2), 8:16, 9:3, 14:2 (x2), 14:5 (x2), 14:10, 14:14, 14:20 (x4), 14:21 (x3), 14:22 (x3), 15:2, 15:14 (x2), 15:21 (x2), 15:22 (x2), 15:23 (x2), 15:24 (x2), 15:25 (x3), 15:27, 15:28, 15:29 (x2), 15:30 (x3), 15:31 (x2), 15:32 (x3), 15:33, 17:5, 21:19 (x3), 21:20 (x3), 21:30, 21:31 (x4), 21:32, 21:33 (x3), 27:8 (x2), 27:9 (x2), 27:10 (x2), 27:23 (x2), 28:3, 28:4 (x2), 28:10 (x2), 28:11, 29:12, 30:24 (x2), 31:20 (x2), 31:29, 31:30, 33:18 (x2 – in one case *nephesh* "his soul" > "them"), 33:19, 33:20 (x2), 33:21 (x2), 33:22 (x2 – in one case *nephesh* "his soul" > "they"), 33:23, 33:24 (x2), 33:25 (x2), 33:26 (x2), 33:27, 33:30 (*nephesh* "his soul" > "them"), 34:11 (x2), 37:7, 40:11, 40:12; **Ps.** 1:3 (x2), 7:14, 7:15 (x2), 7:16 (x4), 8:4 (x2), 8:5 (x2), 8:6 (x2), 10:3 (x3), 10:4 (x2), 10:5 (x4), 10:6 (x2), 10:7 (x2), 10:8 (x2), 10:9 (x4), 10:11, 10:13 (x2), 10:15, 12:2, 15:2, 15:3 (x2), 15:5, 24:5 (x2), 25:12, 32:2, 32:6, 34:19, 34:20, 36:1, 36:2 (x4), 36:3 (x2), 36:4 (x3), 37:24 (x2), 37:30, 37:31 (x3), 37:36 (x3), 40:4, 41:1, 41:2 (x3), 41:3 (x3), 41:6 (x4), 49:12, 49:16, 49:17 (x4), 49:18 (x3), 49:19 (x2), 50:18, 50:23, 53:1, 55:12, 64:4, 91:14 (x3), 91:15 (x5), 91:16 (x2), 94:13, 101:5, 101:6, 103:15 (x2), 104:23 (x2), 107:43, 109:31, 112:2, 112:2, 112:3 (x2), 112:3 (x2), 112:5 (x2), 112:6, 112:7, 112:8 (x4), 112:9 (x3), 112:10 (x2), 126:6 (x2), 129:7 (x2), 137:8, 137:9, 144:3 (x2), 144:4, 146:5 (x2); **Prov.** 3:31, 5:22 (x3), 5:23 (x2), 6:13 (x3), 6:14 (x2), 6:15 (x2), 9:8 (x2), 9:9 (x2), 10:1, 10:19, 10:24, 10:26, 11:9, 11:12, 11:17 (2x), 11:19, 11:27, 11:28, 11:29, 12:8, 12:10, 12:11, 12:14, 12:15, 12:16, 12:27, 13:3 (x2), 13:8, 13:24 (x3), 14:14, 14:15, 14:21 (x2), 14:26, 15:12, 15:20, 15:27, 15:32, 16:2, 16:7 (x2), 16:9 (2x), 16:17 (x2), 16:23 (x2), 16:26 (x3), 16:27, 16:29 (x2), 16:30 (x2), 17:11, 17:25 (x2),

17:28 (x2), 18:2, 18:6, 18:7 (x3), 18:20 (2x), 19:3 (x2), 19:4, 19:7 (x3), 19:8, 19:15 (x2), 19:17 (x2), 19:18, 19:24 (x2), 19:25, 20:2, 20:7 (x2), 20:11 (x2), 20:24, 21:2, 21:10 (x2), 21:11, 21:13, 21:23 (x3), 21:24, 21:25 (x2), 21:26, 21:29, 22:5, 22:6 (x3), 22:8, 22:9 (x3), 22:11, 22:16, 22:25, 22:29 (x3), 23:9, 23:13 (x2), 23:14 (x2), 24:7, 24:12, 24:15, 24:16, 24:17, 24:18, 24:29 (x3), 26:4 (x2), 26:5 (x3), 26:11, 26:12 (x2), 26:15 (x3), 26:16, 26:17, 26:24 (x4), 26:25 (x3), 26:26, 26:27 (x2), 27:18, 27:21, 27:22 (x2), 28:7, 28:10, 28:11 (x2), 28:13, 28:14, 28:17, 28:19 (x2), 28:22, 28:24, 28:26, 28:27, 29:4, 29:5 (x2), 29:11, 29:15, 29:17 (x2), 29:19, 29:20, 29:24 (x2), 30:10 (x2); **Eccl.** 1:3 (x2), 2:14, 2:19, 2:21 (x2), 2:22, 2:23 (x3), 2:24, 3:9, 3:13, 3:22 (x4), 4:4, 4:5, 4:10 (x3), 5:11, 5:12 (x2), 5:14 (x2), 5:15 (x7), 5:16 (x3), 5:17 (x2), 5:18 (x3), 5:19 (x3), 5:20 (x2), 6:2 (x2), 6:12 (x2), 7:15 (x2), 8:15, 8:17, 9:12, 10:3, 10:12, 10:13, 10:14 (x2), 10:15 (x2), 10:15, 11:8 (x3), 12:5; **Isa.** 2:22 (x2), 9:19 (x2), 9:20, 13:14 (x2), 17:5, 19:14, 25:4, 28:4, 28:24 (x2), 28:25 (x3), 28:26 (x3), 29:8 (x3), 29:11, 29:12, 32:6 (x2), 32:7, 32:8, 33:15 (x3), 33:16 (x2), 36:16 (x2), 40:20, 41:24, 44:5, 44:7 (x3), 44:11, 44:20 (x3), 45:9, 46:7 (x2), 50:8, 50:10 (x2), 55:7 (x3), 56:2, 56:3, 56:11, 57:17 (x3), 57:18 (x4), 58:5, 58:7, 65:20; **Jer.** 6:3, 8:4, 8:6, 9:8 (x4), 9:23 (x3), 10:14, 10:23 (x2), 16:12, 17:5, 17:6 (x3), 17:8, 17:10 (x2), 17:11 (x3), 21:9 (x2), 23:14, 23:24, 31:30 (x2), 31:34, 32:19 (x2), 34:9, 34:14 (x2), 36:3, 36:7, 38:2 (x3), 48:10 (x3), 50:16 (x2), 50:17 (x2), 50:19 (x3), 51:17; **Lam.** 3:27, 3:28 (x2), 3:29 (x2), 3:30 (x3), 3:39; **Ezek.** 3:18 (x5), 3:19 (x5), 3:20 (x8), 3:21 (x3), 7:13, 14:7 (x3), 18:20 (x2), 18:21 (x3), 18:22 (x4), 18:24 (x6), 18:26 (x4), 18:27 (x3), 18:28 (x4), 33:5 (x5), 33:8 (x4), 33:9 (x4), 33:12, 33:13 (x6), 33:14 (x2), 33:15 (x3), 33:16 (x4), 33:18 (x2), 33:19 (x2), 34:12 (x2), 47:23 (x2); **Hos.** 12:7; **Amos** 2:9 (x3) ; **Mic.** 2:2 (x2), 2:11, 5:5, 5:6; **Hab.** 2:4, 2:18 (x2); **Zech.** 1:21, 11:6 (x2), 13:3 (x5), 13:4, 13:6 10

**1a. Instances involving the singular Hebrew noun
nephesh, which is grammatically feminine in form and
therefore in some instances is accompanied by feminine verbs and pronouns. At other times the sentence
reverts to masculine verbs and pronouns indicating
that a representative male person is in view. In both
cases the TNIV inappropriately changes singulars to
plurals. (18 inaccuracies)**

Examples:

<u>Leviticus 23:29</u>
NIV: <u>Anyone</u> who does not deny <u>himself</u> on that day must
be cut off from <u>his</u> people.

TNIV: <u>Those</u> who do not deny <u>themselves</u> on that day
must be cut off from <u>their</u> people.

<u>Numbers 19:20</u>
NIV: But if <u>a person</u> who is unclean does not purify <u>him-
self, he</u> must be cut off from the community, because <u>he</u>
has defiled the sanctuary of the LORD. The water of
cleansing has not been sprinkled on <u>him</u>, and <u>he</u> is unclean.

TNIV: But if <u>those</u> who are unclean do not purify <u>them-
selves, they</u> must be cut off from the community, because
<u>they</u> have defiled the sanctuary of the LORD. The water
of cleansing has not been sprinkled on <u>them</u>, and
<u>they</u> are unclean.

Complete List:
Exod. 31:14; **Lev.** 17:10 (x2), 23:29 (x2), 23:30; **Num.**
15:31 (x3), 19:20 (x4); **Ps.** 25:13 (x2), 49:18 (x3)

1b. Changing other words from singular to plural (If a verse listed here also appears in another list, this list only counts those examples in the verse which were not counted when the same verse was listed in the other category.) (291 inaccuracies)

Examples:

Proverbs 12:15
NIV: The way of a <u>fool</u> seems right to <u>him</u>, but a <u>wise man</u> listens to advice.

TNIV: The way of <u>fools</u> seems right to <u>them</u>, but <u>the wise</u> listen to advice.

Ecclesiastes 2:14
NIV: The <u>wise man</u> has eyes in <u>his head</u>, while <u>the fool</u> walks in the darkness; but I came to realize that the same fate overtakes them both.

TNIV: The <u>wise</u> have eyes in <u>their heads</u>, while <u>fools</u> walk in the darkness; but I came to realize that the same fate overtakes them both.

Complete List:
Exod. 4:11 (x2); **Lev.** 7:20, 19:13, 19:33, 19:34, 27:29; **Num.** 12:6, 19:19 (x2), 19:20 (*'ish* "a person" >"those"); **Deut.** 10:18, 14:21, 29:19, 29:20; **Josh.** 2:19 (x2); **Ezra** 2:1; **Neh.** 5:13; **Job** 3:19, 4:17 (*'enosh* "man" > "human beings"), 7:1, 7:10, 9:3, 14:2, 14:22, 15:2 (x2), 15:14, 15:25, 17:5, 21:30, 28:3, 30:24, 31:29, 33:19, 33:20, 33:22, 33:23, 33:27 (x2), 33:28 (x2), 40:11, 40:12; **Ps.** 7:16, 8:6, 10:3, 10:6, 10:7 (x2), 10:9, 10:13, 10:15 (x2), 15:2 (x2), 15:3 (x2), 15:5, 32:2, 34:19, 37:30 (x3), 37:31, 41:1, 84:12, 119:9;

Prov. 8:36 (x2), 11:8, 11:13 (x2), 11:18 (x2), 11:19 (x2), 11:26 (x2), 11:28, 11:29, 11:30, 12:2 (x2), 12:13 (x2), 12:15 (x2), 12:16 (x2), 12:23, 12:27, 13:3 (x3), 13:8 (x3), 13:16 (x2), 14:2, 14:29 (x2), 16:13, 16:20 (x2), 16:23 (x3), 16:30 (x2), 16:32 (x2), 17:11, 17:16, 17:23 (x2), 17:27 (x2), 18:2, 18:6, 18:7 (x3), 18:23 (x2), 19:1, 19:8 (x3), 19:15, 19:16 (x3), 19:17, 19:24 (x3), 19:25, 20:2 (x2), 20:4 (x2), 20:11, 21:10 (x2), 21:13, 21:20, 21:23 (x3), 21:25, 22:3, 22:5, 22:6, 22:8, 22:24 (x2), 23:9, 23:13, 24:7, 24:16, 25:26, 26:4, 26:5, 26:11, 26:15 (x3), 26:16, 26:24 (x2), 27:22, 28:6 (x2), 28:7 (x2), 28:10, 28:11, 28:13 (x2), 28:14 (x3), 28:19 (x2), 28:25 (x2), 28:26 (x3), 28:27 (x2), 29:5 (x3 – in one case *geber* "whoever" > "those who"), 29:6 (x2), 29:11 (x2), 29:15 (x2), 29:18, 29:24 (x3); **Eccl.** 2:14 (x3), 3:9, 4:5 (x2), 5:11, 5:12 (x2), 6:2, 6:8 (x3), 10:3 (x2), 10:12 (x2), 10:14; **Isa.** 19:14, 28:24, 31:3 (x2), 32:6 (x2), 32:7, 32:8 (x2), 33:15 (x2), 40:20, 45:9, 45:10, 50:8, 56:3, 66:2 (x2); **Jer.** 9:8 (x2), 9:24, 17:5, 17:11 (x3), 23:28 (x3), 48:10 (x2); **Lam.** 3:29, 3:30, 3:39; **Ezek.** 6:12 (x3), 18:21, 18:24 (x2), 18:26, 18:27, 20:11, 20:13, 33:5, 33:8 (x2), 33:9, 33:13, 33:14, 33:18, 33:19, 34:12 (x2), 47:23; **Hos.** 12:7; **Amos** 2:9, 5:11, 5:13; **Mic.** 2:11 (x3), 5:5, 5:6; **Zech.** 1:21, 8:10, 11:6, 13:3

2. Changing "he/him/his" to "they" used with singular English antecedent

Comment: These changes produce sentences where it is unclear whether a singular or plural is intended. The sentences use "they" in a so-called "singular" sense, which is often heard in ordinary conversation but widely criticized by English style manuals (the AP Style Manual, the American Heritage Dictionary, Strunk and White, William Zinsser) as something inappropriate for written English. But whatever people choose to do with their own compositions today, it is still inappropriate to translate these third person masculine singular pronouns and verbs in the Bible with "they" rather than "he," because "he" best translates what the Hebrew text actually says. (474 inaccuracies)

Examples:

Numbers 6:9
NIV: If someone dies suddenly in his presence, thus defiling the hair <u>he</u> has dedicated, <u>he</u> must shave <u>his</u> head on the day of <u>his</u> cleansing—the seventh day.

TNIV: If someone dies suddenly in the Nazirite's presence, thus defiling the hair that symbolizes <u>their</u> dedication, <u>they</u> must shave <u>their</u> head on the seventh day—the day of <u>their</u> cleansing.

Deuteronomy 23:15-16
NIV: If a slave has taken refuge with you, do not hand <u>him</u> over to <u>his</u> master. Let <u>him</u> live among you wherever <u>he</u> likes and in whatever town <u>he</u> chooses. Do not oppress <u>him</u>.

TNIV: If a slave has taken refuge with you, do not hand <u>them</u> over to <u>their</u> master. Let <u>them</u> live among you wherever <u>they</u> like and in whatever town <u>they</u> choose. Do not oppress <u>them</u>.

Complete List:
Exod. 16:16, 16:18, 19:13 (x3), 21:13, 21:17, 21:20, 21:21 (x2), 22:3 (x3), 22:4 (x2), 22:5, 30:33, 30:38, 33:10, 35:21; **Lev.** 4:27, 4:28 (x4), 4:29 (x2), 4:31 (x3), 4:32 (x3), 4:33

(x2), 4:35 (x4), 5:3 (x5), 5:4 (x3), 5:5 (x2), 5:6 (x4), 5:7 (x3), 5:8, 5:10 (x3), 5:11 (x4), 5:12, 5:13 (x3), 5:16 (x4), 5:18 (x4), 5:19, 6:3 (x2), 6:4 (x5), 6:5 (x4), 6:6 (x2), 6:7 (x3), 7:12 (x2), 7:13 (x2), 7:14, 7:15 (x2), 7:16 (x2), 7:29, 7:30 (x2), 11:25 (x2), 11:28 (x2), 11:40 (x4), 13:2 (x2), 13:3 (x2), 13:5 (x2), 13:6 (x5), 13:7 (x3), 13:8, 13:9, 13:11 (x3), 13:13 (x2), 13:14 (x2), 13:15 (x2), 13:16, 13:17 (x2), 13:18, 13:19, 13:20, 13:21, 13:22, 13:23, 13:24, 13:25, 13:26, 13:27 (x2), 13:28, 13:33, 13:34 (x3), 13:35 (x4), 13:36, 13:37 (x2), 13:45, 13:46 (x3), 14:2 (x2), 14:7, 14:8 (x6), 14:9 (x11), 14:10, 14:14 (x2), 14:17 (x2), 14:18, 14:19, 14:20 (x2), 14:21 (x3), 14:22, 14:23 (x2), 14:25 (x2), 14:28 (x2), 14:29, 14:32, 14:47, 15:5 (x2), 15:6 (x2), 15:7 (x2), 15:8 (x2), 15:10 (x2), 15:11 (x2), 15:21 (x2), 15:22 (x3), 15:27 (x3), 17:15 (x3), 17:16 (x3), 19:17, 20:9 (x5), 24:15, 24:16 (x3), 25:25 (x3), 25:35 (x3), 25:36, 25:37, 25:39, 25:40 (x2), 25:41 (x5), 25:48 (x5), 25:49 (x5), 25:50 (x5), 25:51 (x3), 25:52 (x2), 25:53 (x2), 25:54 (x3), 27:14, 27:15 (x3), 27:16, 27:17, 27:19 (x2), 27:20 (x2), 27:22 (x2); **Num.** 1:52 (x2), 2:2, 2:17, 2:34, 5:7 (x3), 6:3 (x2), 6:4 (x2), 6:5 (x4), 6:6, 6:7 (x5), 6:8 (x2), 6:9 (x4), 6:10, 6:11 (x3), 6:12 (x4), 6:13, 6:14 (x2), 6:18 (x2), 6:19, 6:21 (x4), 15:14, 15:28 (x2), 19:12 (x6), 19:13 (x5), 19:19 (x3), 21:9, 35:20 (x2), 35:21, 35:22, 35:23 (x2), 35:25; **Deut.** 4:42 (x3), 12:8, 15:2 (x2), 15:9 (x2), 15:10, 15:13 (x2), 15:14 (x2), 18:10, 19:15, 21:22, 22:3, 23:7, 23:15, 23:16 (x4), 24:15 (x3), 25:2 (x2), 27:16, 27:17; **Josh.** 20:4 (x5), 20:5 (x3), 20:6 (x5), 24:28; **Jdg.** 2:6, 17:6; **1 Sam.** 2:25; **2 Sam.** 14:10 (x2), 15:4; **1 Kgs.** 4:25, 8:31 (x2), 8:32 (x3), 8:38 (x2), 8:39 (x2); **2 Kgs.** 23:10; **2 Chron.** 6:22 (x2), 6:23 (x3), 6:29 (x2), 6:30 (x2), 30:19 (x2), 36:23 (x3); **Prov.** 11:28, 12:16, 28:9, 29:20; **Jer.** 12:15 (x2);**Ezek.** 3:27 (x2), 7:16, 14:4 (x4), 14:7 (x4), 14:8 (x2), 33:4 (x3), 33:6 (x2), 46:18; **Hos.** 14:9 (x2); **Mic.** 4:4 (x2)

2a. Instances involving the singular Heb. noun *nephesh,* which is grammatically feminine in form and therefore in some instances is accompanied by feminine verbs and pronouns. At other times the sentence reverts to masculine verbs and pronouns indicating that a representative male person is in view. In both cases the TNIV inappropriately changes singulars to plurals. (This is similar to category 1a above, except here the TNIV has used "they" with a singular antecedent in English, and in category 1a the antecedent was plural.) (27 inaccuracies)

Examples:

Leviticus 5:1
NIV: If a <u>person</u> sins because <u>he</u> does not speak up when <u>he</u> hears a public charge to testify regarding something <u>he</u> has seen or learned about, <u>he</u> will be held responsible.

TNIV: If <u>anyone</u> sins because <u>they</u> do not speak up when <u>they</u> hear a public charge to testify regarding something <u>they</u> have seen or learned about, <u>they</u> will be held responsible.

Numbers 9:13
NIV: But if a man who is ceremonially clean and not on a journey fails to celebrate the Passover, <u>that person</u> must be cut off from <u>his</u> people because he did not present the LORD's offering at the appointed time. <u>That man</u> will bear the consequences of <u>his</u> sin.

TNIV: But if anyone who is ceremonially clean and not on a journey fails to celebrate the Passover, <u>they</u> must be cut off from <u>their</u> people for not presenting the LORD's offering at the appointed time. <u>They</u> will bear the consequences of <u>their</u> sin.

Complete List:
Lev. 5:1 (x4), 5:2 (x2), 5:15, 5:17 (x2), 6:2 (x2), 7:20, 7:21, 7:25, 7:27, 19:8 (x2), 20:6 (x3); **Num.** 9:13 (x2), 15:30, 19:20 (x4)

3. Changing the 3rd person singular pronoun "he/him/his/himself" to second person "you/your/yours/yourself" (64 inaccuracies)

Comment: There is no question that the Hebrew pronouns and verbs are third person masculine singular ("he"). But here the TNIV has changed "he" to "you," which does not accurately represent what the Hebrew text says. In a number of cases the focus is changed from a general case "out there" (using "he") to a specific address to the readers or hearers ("you"), and thus the meaning is changed to something that God did not say. In these verses the TNIV is not translating with the nearest English equivalent but is trying to translate while avoiding the "taboo" words "he/him/his," and an inaccurate translation is the result.

Examples:

<u>Deuteronomy 24:16</u>
NIV: Fathers shall not be put to death for their children, nor children put to death for their fathers; each is to die for <u>his</u> own sin.

TNIV: Parents are not to be put to death for their

children, nor children put to death for their parents; each
of you will die for your own sin.

Complete List:
Exod. 12:22; **Lev.** 1:3 (x2), 1:4 (x4), 1:5, 1:6, 1:9, 1:10,
1:11, 1:12, 1:13, 1:14, 2:1 (x2), 3:1 (x2), 3:2 (x3), 3:3, 3:4,
3:6 (x2), 3:7 (x2), 3:8, 3:9, 3:10, 3:12 (x2), 3:13, 3:14 (x2),
3:15, 19:3, 25:10 (x2); **Deut.** 24:16; **2 Sam.** 20:1; **1 Kgs.**
22:36 (x2); **2 Kgs.** 14:6 (x2), 18:31 (x2); **2 Chron.** 25:4; **Ps.**
52:6, 54:7; **Prov.** 5:21, 20:20 (x2); **Ecc.** 7:14 (changes "a
man" to "you"); **Isa.** 29:16 (x2); **Jer.** 34:15; **Ezek.** 18:30,
33:20; **Mic.** 3:5 (x2), 7:6; **Zech.** 3:10

4. Changing the 3rd person singular "he/him/his/ himself" to "we/our/ourselves" (8 inaccuracies)

Comment: As in category 3, there is no question that the
Hebrew pronouns and verbs are third person masculine
singular ("he"). But here the TNIV has changed "he" to
"we/our/ourselves," which does not accurately represent
what the Hebrew text says. In a number of cases the focus is changed from a general case "out there" (using "he")
to a specific statement about the writer and his hearers
("we"), and thus the meaning is changed to something that
God did not say. As in category 3, in these verses also the
TNIV is not translating with the nearest English equivalent but is trying to translate while avoiding the "taboo"
words "he/him/his," and an inaccurate translation is the
result.

Examples:

<u>Job 14:6</u>
NIV: So look away from <u>him</u> and let <u>him</u> alone, till <u>he</u> has put in <u>his</u> time like a hired man.

TNIV: So look away from <u>us</u> and leave <u>us</u> alone, till <u>we</u> have put in <u>our</u> time like hired laborers.

Complete List:
Neh. 4:15; **Job** 14:6 (x4); **Is.** 53:6; **Jer.** 18:12, 51:9

5. Changing whoever/anyone/one/everyone (singular) to "those" or "those who" (plural) (13 inaccuracies)

Comment: This is another example of the TNIV changing singulars to plurals just to avoid the word "he/him/his," again changing the emphasis in these verses from individual persons to groups that are responsible to God and that relate to God.

Examples:

<u>Exodus 31:14</u>
NIV: Observe the Sabbath, because it is holy to you. Anyone who desecrates it must be put to death; <u>whoever</u> does any work on that day must be cut off from his people.

TNIV: Observe the Sabbath, because it is holy to you. Anyone who desecrates it is to be put to death; <u>those who</u> do any work on that day must be cut off from their people.

Ecclesiastes 5:10

NIV: <u>Whoever</u> loves money never has money enough; <u>whoever</u> loves wealth is never satisfied with his income. This too is meaningless.

TNIV: <u>Those who</u> love money never have enough; <u>those who</u> love wealth are never satisfied with their income. This too is meaningless.

Complete List:
Exod. 31:14; **Lev.** 23:29; **Josh.** 2:19; **Prov.** 8:35, 8:36, 14:2, 16:20, 21:23, 28:13, 28:19 (x2); **Eccl.** 5:10 (x2)

6. Completely removing the 3rd person singular pronoun "he/him/his/himself" (and often rewording the sentence in various other ways) (255 inaccuracies)

Comment: In these verses the words "he/him/his" are simply omitted, and thus part of the meaning that was there in the original text is deleted or changed to something the text did not say.

Examples:

Exodus 21:12

NIV: Anyone who strikes a man and <u>kills him</u> shall surely be put to death.

TNIV: Anyone who strikes <u>someone a fatal blow</u> is to be put to death.

1 Samuel 2:25

NIV: If a man sins against another man, God may mediate

for <u>him</u>; but if a man sins against the LORD, who will intercede for him?" His sons, however, did not listen to their father's rebuke, for it was the LORD's will to put them to death.

TNIV: If anyone sins against another human being, God may mediate for <u>the offender</u>; but if anyone sins against the LORD, who will intercede for them?" His sons, however, did not listen to their father's rebuke, for it was the LORD's will to put them to death.

Psalm 1:2
NIV: But <u>his</u> delight is in the law of the LORD, and on his law <u>he</u> meditates day and night.

TNIV: but <u>who</u> delight in the law of the LORD and meditate on his law day and night.

Nahum 2:2-3
NIV: The LORD will restore the splendor of Jacob like the splendor of Israel, though destroyers have laid them waste and have ruined their vines. The shields of <u>his</u> soldiers are red; the warriors are clad in scarlet…

TNIV: The LORD will restore the splendor of Jacob like the splendor of Israel, though destroyers have laid them waste and have ruined their vines. The shields of <u>the</u> soldiers are red; the warriors are clad in scarlet…

Complete List:
Gen. 6:5 ["the human"], 9:27 ["of Japheth"], 26:31 [removed], 31:32 ["that one"]; **Exod.** 21:12 ["kills him" > "strikes a fatal blow"], 21:13 ["he does not do it" > "it is not done"], 21:14 ["take him away" > "person is to be

taken"], 21:16 [x2 – "sells him" > "has been sold"; "still has him" > "is still in the kidnapper's possession"], 21:18 ["the victim"], 21:19 [x4 – "a"; "the guilty party"; "any loss"; "the victim"], 21:20 [removed], 21:26 [removed], 21:27 [x2 – "an owner"; removed], 21:30 [x3 – removed; "he may redeem his life" > "the owner's life may be redeemed"], 21:34 [x2 – removed; "will be his" > "in exchange"], 21:36 ["will be his" > "in exchange"], 22:1 [removed], 22:3 ["the defender"], 22:5 [x2 – "he must make restitution" > "restitution must be made"; "the livestock owner's"], 22:7 [x2 – "a"; removed], 22:8 [x2 – "the owner of the house"; removed], 22:9 ["his neighbor" > "the other"], 22:10 ["a"], 22:12 ["he must make restitution" > "restitution must be made"], 22:13 [x2 – "the neighbor"; removed], 22:14 [x2 – "a"; "he must make restitution" > "restitution must be made"], 22:21 [removed], 22:25 [removed], 22:26 [removed], 23:3 ["a"], 23:4 [removed], 33:11 ["a"]; **Lev.** 3:8 [x2 – "he is to lay" > "lay"; "the head of his offering" > "its head"], 3:13 ["he is to lay" > "lay"], 5:7 [x2 – "if he" > "anyone who"; removed], 6:2 ["a"], 6:3 ["if he commits any such sin" > "any such sin that people may commit"], 20:9 [x2 – "he must be" > "is to be"; removed], 22:14 [removed], 24:15 [removed], 24:17 ["he must be" > "is to be"], 24:19 [x3 – "a"; "whatever he has done must be done to him" > "is to be injured in the same manner"], 24:20 [x2 – "As he has injured the other, so he is to be injured" > "The one who has inflicted the injury must suffer the same injury"], 25:16 ["what he is really selling you" > "what is really being sold to you"], 25:28 [x2 – removed; "what he sold" > "what was sold"], 25:30 ["the buyer's"], 27:8 [x2 – "he is to present the person" > "the person being dedicated is to be presented"; removed], 27:13 ["he must add" > "must be added"], 27:17 ["a"], 27:18 ["a"], 27:24 ["he bought" > "was bought"], 27:27 [x2 – "he may buy" > "may be bought"; "he does not redeem" > "is not redeemed"], 27:33 [x2 – "no one"; "anyone"]; **Num.** 5:8 ["the wrongdoer"], 5:10 ["are his own" > "belong to the donors"], 6:5 ["the Nazarite's"], 6:6 ["the Nazarite"], 6:9 ["the Nazarite's"], 6:11 ["the Nazarite"], 6:12 ["period of his separation" > "the same period of dedication"], 6:13 ["the Nazarite"], 6:21 [removed], 9:13 ["because he did not present" > "for not presenting"], 15:4 ["an"], 35:16 [x2 – "so that he dies" > "a fatal blow"; "that person"], 35:17 [x2 – "so that he dies" > "a fatal blow"; "that person"], 35:18 [x2 – "so that he dies" > "a fatal blow"; "that per-son"], 35:19 [x4 – "the avenger"; "the murderer"; "the avenger"; "the murderer"], 35:21 [x5 – "one person"; "an-other"; "the other"; "that person"; "he meets him" > "they meet"], 35:23 [x3 – "that other person"; "an"; "he did not intend to harm him" > "no harm was intended"], 35:25 [x2 – "the accused" (both)], 35:27 ["that person"], 35:28 [x2 – "the"; "his own property" > "home"], 35:31 ["a murderer"]; **Deut.** 4:42 ["a"], 13:2 ["he has spoken" > "spoken of"], 13:5 ["because he preached" > "for incit-ing"], 15:2 ["another"], 17:7 ["that person"], 18:19 [rear-ranges entire sentence structure to remove], 18:22 ["do not be afraid of him." > "no one should be alarmed"], 19:4 ["a"], 19:11 [x3 – "man hates his neighbor" > "out of hate someone"; removed; "a neighbor"], 19:12 [x3 – "elders of <u>his</u> town shall send for <u>him</u>" > "killer shall be sent for by the town elders"; "hand him" > "be handed"], 19:13 [re-moved], 19:19 [x3 – "the false witness"; "that witness"; "his brother" > "the other party"], 20:8 ["his brothers" > "the others"], 21:1 ["who killed him" > "who the killer was"], 21:23 [x2 – "the"; "it"], 22:2 ["who he is" > "who owns it"], 22:3 [removed], 22:4 [x2 – removed; "the owner"], 23:7 ["he is your brother" > "the Edomites are related to you"], 24:7 ["treats him as a slave or sells him"

> "treating or selling that Israelite as a slave"], 24:10 [x2 – "the neighbor's"; "what he is offering" > "what is offered to you"], 24:12 ["that"], 24:13 [x3 – removed; "your neighbor"; "he will thank you" > "you will be thanked"], 25:2 ["the"], 25:3 [x2 – "the judge"; "the guilty party"], 27:16 [removed], 29:19 [removed], 32:5 [removed (N.B. "him" refers to God)]; **Josh.** 7:17 ["he took" > "were chosen" (N.B. "he" refers to God)], 8:29 ["the"]; **Ruth** 4:16 ["laid him in her lap" > "in her arms"]; **1 Sam.** 2:25 ["the offender"]; **2 Sam.** 1:6 ["almost upon him" > "in hot pursuit"]; **2 Kgs.** 3:11 ["whom" (N.B. the wording has been modified)], 11:8 [x2 – removed (both)], 11:11 [x2 – removed (both)]; **2 Chron.** 23:7 [x2 – removed (both)]; **Job** 6:14 [x2 – removed], 9:33 ["a"], 16:21 ["a"], 21:24 [x2 – "in"; removed], 24:14 [removed], 33:26 ["his righteous state" > "full well being"]; **Ps.** 1:2 [x2 – "who"; removed], 10:10 ["superior"], 10:11 ["the wicked"], 15:3 ["his fellowman" > "others"], 15:5 [removed], 38:13 ["open his mouth" > "speak"], 41:2 [removed], 49:7 ["ransom for him" > "sufficient ransom"], 49:9 ["someone"], 50:23 [x2 – removed (both)], 62:4 ["my"], 81:5 ["God"], 89:48 ["save himself from" > "who can escape"], 101:5 [x2 – removed], 109:6 ["my enemy"]; **Prov.** 12:27 ["any"], 14:21 ["He who despises his neighbor sins," > "It is a sin to despise one's neighbor,"], 16:2 [removed], 16:32 ["man who controls his temper" > "those with self control"], 17:12 ["in his folly" > "bent on folly"], 17:13 ["the"], 17:18 ["a"], 18:1 [removed (N.B. the wording has been modified)], 18:16 ["the giver"], 18:17 [x2 – removed (N.B. the wording has been modified); "questions him" > "cross-examines"], 19:3 [x2 – "ruins his life" > "leads to ruin"; "the"], 19:11 ["gives him" > "yields"], 19:13 ["a"], 19:24 [removed], 20:16 ["he does it" > "it is done"], 21:13 [removed], 22:15 ["from him" > "away"], 24:24 [x2 – "curse

him… denounce him" > "be cursed…and denounced"],
25:17 ["he will hate you" > "you will be hated"], 25:18
["a"], 26:14 ["the"], 26:15 [removed], 26:19 ["a"], 27:8
[removed], 27:14 ["a"], 28:24 [removed], 29:21 [x2 –
"pampers his servant" > "a servant pampered"; removed
(N.B. the wording has been modified)], 29:23 ["a person"],
30:4 ["whose" (N.B. the wording has been modified); "a"],
30:31 ["with his army around him" > "secure against re-
volt"]; **Eccl.** 2:19 ["whether he will be a wise man or a
fool?" > "whether that person will be wise or foolish?"],
6:2 ["enable him" > "grant the ability"], 6:7 ["the"], 6:10
["than he" > "someone"], 8:6 ["a man's misery weighs
heavily upon him" > "a person may be weighed down by
misery"], 8:7 ["tell him" > "say"] 8:16 ["his eyes not seeing
sleep" > "people getting no sleep"]; **Song** 8:7 ["one's"];
Isa. 7:22 ["he will have" > "there will be"], 9:19 ["his
brother" > "each other"], 28:4 [removed], 28:28 [x2 – re-
moved], 29:16 ["the one"], 41:7 ["the other"], 45:9 ["the
potter"], 50:9 [removed]; **Jer.** 31:34 ["a man his brother,
saying," > "say to one another"]; **Ezek.** 9:1 [removed],
33:12 [x3 – removed (all, but N.B. the wording of the
verse has been considerably modified)], 39:15 [removed];
Dan. 7:1 [removed (N.B. Aramaic)]; **Amos** 3:11 [re-
moved]; **Nah.** 2:3 [removed (N.B. "his" refers to God)];
Zech. 4:1 [removed], 5:4 ["that"], 8:10 ["his neighbor" >
"each other"], 13:5 ["every one of them"], 13:6 [removed];
Mal. 2:16 ["a man's covering himself with violence as well
as with his garment" > "people clothe themselves with
injustice"]

7. Completely omitting other words that are represented in Hebrew and translated in the NIV but simply removed from the TNIV (13 inaccuracies)

Examples:

Leviticus 7:27
NIV: If anyone eats blood, <u>that person</u> must be cut off from his people.

TNIV: Anyone who eats blood must be cut off from their people.

Psalm 55:12
NIV: If an enemy were insulting me, I could endure it; if a foe were raising himself against me, I could <u>hide from him</u>.

TNIV: If an enemy were insulting me, I could endure it; if a foe were rising against me, I could <u>hide</u>.

Complete List:
Lev. 7:21 [omit "that person" *nephesh*], 7:27 [omit "that person" (*nephesh*)], 17:9 [omit "that man" *'ish*], 17:10 [omit "that person" (the verse is rearranged to omit the phrase)]; **Num.** 15:30 [omit "that person"], 16:14 ["Will you gouge out the eyes of these men?" > "Do you want to treat these men like slaves"]; **1 Sam.** 2:21 ["she conceived and gave birth" > "she gave birth"]; **Ps.** 55:12 [omit "from him"]; **Eccl.** 4:10 ["his companion" > "they"], 6:10 [omits "than he"]; **Isa.** 25:10 ["under him" > "in their land"]; **Ezek.** 5:2 [omit "with fire"]; **Nah.** 3:13 ["women" > "weaklings"]

B. Changes Made to Avoid the Word "Father"

8. Changing singular *'ab* "father" to "parent" or "parents" (19 inaccuracies)

Comment: There are no cases where the singular Hebrew word *'ab* means "parent" rather than "father" and Hebrew lexicons define this word in singular as "father," not as "parent" (see Brown-Driver-Briggs, *Hebrew and English Lexicon of the Old Testament,* p. 3; also Koehler-Baumgartner, *Hebrew and Aramaic Lexicon of the Old Testament,* pp. 1-2). But the TNIV translators in these verses were unwilling to translate the word with the clear, simple English equivalent "father," apparently because in today's culture it is unpopular to use an example of an individual father to teach a general truth that applies to all parents. Even when that is what the Hebrew text does, the TNIV is unwilling to allow English readers today to see it. Rather than translating the word *'ab* in these verses the TNIV is avoiding translating it. It is a "taboo" word that must be avoided in these contexts that teach a general truth.

Examples:

Proverbs 13:1
NIV: A wise son heeds his <u>father's</u> instruction, but a mocker does not listen to rebuke.

TNIV: A wise child heeds a <u>parent's</u> instruction, but a mocker does not respond to rebukes.

Proverbs 15:5
NIV: A fool spurns his <u>father's</u> discipline, but whoever

heeds correction shows prudence.

TNIV: A fool spurns a <u>parent's</u> discipline, but whoever heeds correction shows prudence.

Complete List:
Josh. 15:13, 19:47, 21:11; **Neh.** 1:6; **Prov.** 13:1, 15:5, 17:21, 27:10, 28:7; **Isa.** 38:19; **Jer.** 35:6, 35:8, 35:10, 35:14, 35:16, 35:18; **Ezek.** 18:4, 18:20 (x2)

9. Changing plural *'aboth* "fathers" or "forefathers" to "ancestors" (287 inaccuracies)

Comment: The lexicons give "ancestor" as one possible definition (Brown-Driver-Briggs, Hebrew and English Lexicon of the Old Testament, p. 3; also Koehler-Baumgartner, *Hebrew and Aramaic Lexicon of the Old Testament*, p. 1), but all the specific examples given are men. We have included these verses in this list because they seem to us to fit the general pattern of excluding male nuances in the TNIV, and because the male nuance or connotation of the plural word *'aboth* would have been evident to original Hebrew readers (since it is simply the plural of *'ab*, "father"), and that connection is clearly seen in the English words "fathers" and "forefathers," but the TNIV has removed that male nuance by consistently using the term "ancestors."

Examples:

Joshua 1:6
NIV: Be strong and courageous, because you will lead these people to inherit the land I swore to their <u>forefathers</u>

to give them.

TNIV: Be strong and courageous, because you will lead these people to inherit the land I swore to their ancestors to give them.

1 Kings 2:10
NIV: Then David rested with his fathers and was buried in the City of David.

TNIV: Then David rested with his ancestors and was buried in the City of David.

Daniel 2:23
NIV: I thank and praise you, O God of my fathers: You have given me wisdom and power, you have made known to me what we asked of you, you have made known to us the dream of the king.

TNIV: I thank and praise you, God of my ancestors: You have given me wisdom and power, you have made known to me what we asked of you, you have made known to us the dream of the king.

Complete List:
Gen. 15:15; **Exod.** 10:6 (x2 parents, ancestors), 13:11; **Lev.** 25:41, 26:39, 26:40; **Num.** 11:12, 14:23, 18:1 (ancestral family), 36:4, 36:6, 36:7, 36:8; **Deut.** 1:11, 1:21, 1:35, 4:1, 4:31, 4:37, 5:3, 6:3, 6:18, 6:23, 7:8, 7:12, 7:13, 8:1, 8:3, 8:16, 8:18, 10:11, 10:15, 11:9, 11:21, 12:1, 13:6, 13:17, 19:8, 26:3, 26:7, 26:15, 27:3, 28:11, 28:36, 28:64, 29:25, 30:5 (x2), 31:7, 31:16, 31:20, 32:17; **Josh.** 1:6, 4:21 (parents), 5:6, 18:3, 21:43, 21:44, 24:2, 24:14, 24:15; **Jdg.** 2:1, 2:10, 2:12, 2:17, 2:19, 2:22, 6:13; **1 Sam.** 12:15; **2 Sam.** 7:12; **1 Kgs.**

1:21, 2:10, 8:34, 8:40, 8:48, 8:57, 11:21, 11:43, 13:22, 14:15, 15:12, 15:24, 16:6, 16:28, 21:3, 21:4, 22:40, 22:50; **2 Kgs.** 8:24, 9:28, 10:35, 12:18 (predecessors), 12:21, 13:9, 13:13, 14:16, 14:20, 14:22, 14:29, 15:7 (x2), 15:9, (predecessors), 15:22, 15:38 (x2), 16:20 (x2), 17:13, 17:14, 17:15, 17:41, 19:12, 20:17 (predecessors), 20:21, 21:8, 21:18, 21:22, 22:13 ('those who have gone before us'), 22:20, 23:32 (predecessors), 23:37 (predecessor), 24:6; **1 Chron.** 5:25, 9:19, 12:17, 17:11, 24:19, 29:15; **2 Chron.** 6:25, 6:31, 6:38, 7:22, 9:31, 11:16, 12:16, 13:12, 13:18, 14:1, 14:4, 15:12, 16:13, 19:4, 20:6, 20:33, 21:1, 21:10, 21:19 (predecessors), 24:18, 24:24, 25:28, 26:2, 26:23, 27:9, 28:6, 28:9, 28:25, 28:27, 29:5, 29:6, 29:9, 30:7 (x2 parents, ancestors), 30:8 (parents), 30:19, 30:22, 32:13 (predecessors), 32:14, (predecessors), 32:15 (predecessors), 32:33, 33:8, 33:12, 33:20, 34:21 ('those who have gone before us'), 34:28, 34:32, 34:33, 35:24, 36:15; **Ezra** 5:12, 7:27, 8:28, 9:7, 10:11; **Neh.** 2:5, 9:2, 9:9, 9:16, 9:23, 9:32, 9:34, 9:36, 13:18; **Job** 8:8; **Ps.** 22:4, 44:1, 78:3, 78:5, 78:8, 78:12, 78:57, 95:9, 106:6, 107:7; **Prov.** 22:28; **Isa.** 14:21, 37:12, 39:6 (predecessors), 64:11, 65:7; **Jer.** 2:5, 3:18, 3:24, 3:25, 6:21 (parents), 7:7, 7:14, 7:22, 7:25, 7:26, 9:14, 9:16, 11:4, 11:5, 11:7, 11:10 (x2), 13:14 (parents), 14:20, 16:11, 16:12, 16:13, 16:19, 17:22, 19:4, 23:27, 23:39, 24:10, 25:5, 30:3, 31:29 (parents), 31:32, 32:18 (parents'), 32:22, 34:5, 34:13, 34:14, 35:15, 44:3, 44:9, 44:10, 44:17, 44:21, 47:3 (parents), 50:7; **Lam.** 5:7 (parents); **Ezek.** 2:3, 5:10 (x2 parents), 18:2 (parents), 20:4, 20:18 (parents), 20:24 (parents), 20:27, 20:30, 20:42, 36:28, 37:25, 47:14; **Dan.** 2:23, 9:6, 9:8, 9:16, 11:37, 11:38, **Hos.** 9:10; **Joel** 1:2; **Mic.** 7:20; **Zech.** 1:2, 1:4, 1:5, 1:6, 8:14; **Mal.** 2:10, 3:7, 4:6 (2x) 4

10. Diminishing the role of the father in ancient Israelite society (11 inaccuracies)

Comment: Although the Hebrew text speaks several times of a "father's house" or "father's family" and uses the ordinary Hebrew word for "father" (*'ab*), the TNIV eliminated the word "father" and substituted "family" or some other expression. The new expressions remove any suggestion of a father's leadership role in the family. These TNIV verses are not translated accurately as a result, but these verses are consistent with the TNIV practice of removing male-oriented details of meaning from the text of the Bible.

Examples:

1 Samuel 18:2
NIV: From that day Saul kept David with him and did not let him return to his <u>father's house</u>.

TNIV: From that day Saul kept David with him and did not let him return home to his <u>family</u>.

2 Chronicles 21:13
NIV: But you have walked in the ways of the kings of Israel, and you have led Judah and the people of Jerusalem to prostitute themselves, just as the house of Ahab did. You have also murdered your own brothers, members of your <u>father's</u> house, men who were better than you.

TNIV: But you have followed the ways of the kings of Israel, and you have led Judah and the people of Jerusalem to prostitute themselves, just as the house of Ahab did. You have also murdered your own brothers, members of your <u>own family</u>, men who were better than you.

Complete List:
1 Sam. 2:27, 2:30, 2:31, 9:20, 17:25, 18:2, 22:11; **2 Sam.** 3:29, 14:9; **1 Kgs.** 2:31; **2 Chron.** 21:13

C. Changes Made to Avoid the Word "Brother"

11. Changing "brother" (singular) to another word that has no familial connotation (26 inaccuracies)

Comment: The Hebrew word *'ah* (singular) basically means "brother," either in a narrow sense to mean a male sibling in one's own family or else in a broader sense of a relative or a member of the same tribe or people (a sense the English word "brother" also has). Even when used in a broader sense the word carries a connotation of a family relationship which is reflected in the English word "brother," and this makes "brother" a good translation with a semantic range very close to the Hebrew term. But the TNIV in several verses has changed "brother" to various words that do not have any familial sense, such as "someone" or "fellow Israelite," or has eliminated the word altogether. This makes for a less accurate translation, and it follows the TNIV pattern of inappropriately eliminating many male-oriented words.

In several verses the Hebrew text uses the singular *'ah* ("brother") as a male example to teach a general truth that applies to all people, as in Lev. 19:17, "Do not hate <u>your brother</u> in your heart." But the TNIV will not allow the Bible to use a male example to teach a general truth in verses like this, so the verse has been changed to, "Do not hate <u>a fellow Israelite</u> in your heart" (TNIV; the first instance of the pronoun "your" is not translated at all in the TNIV). The actual word in the Hebrew text means "brother" but the TNIV will not allow the Bible to say "brother" in verses like this.

Examples:

<u>**Deuteronomy 19:18**</u>
NIV: The judges must make a thorough investigation, and if the witness proves to be a liar, giving false <u>testimony against his brother,</u>

TNIV: The judges must make a thorough investigation, and if the witness proves to be a liar, giving false <u>testimony,</u>

Complete List:
Lev. 19:17 (>fellow Israelite); **Deut.** 1:16 (brother>two), 15:2 (his fellow Israelite or brother> anyone among their own people), 15:3 (>one of your people), 15:9 (your needy brother>the needy among your people), 15:11 (brothers>those of your people), 17:15 (brother Israelite>an Israelite), 19:18 (removed!), 19:19 (>the other party), 22:1 (>someone else's), 22:2 (>owner), 22:4 (>someone's), 23:7 (>are related to you [pluralized]), 25:3 (>Israelite neighbor); **2 Sam.** 2:27 (>them); **1 Kgs.** 20:32 (>an old ally), 20:33 (>old ally); **Prov.** 18:9 (>a close relative), 27:10 (x2 – relative/'s) [this change fits the general TNIV pattern of eliminating male examples used to teach a general truth]; **Isa.** 9:19 (>each other), 41:6 (his brother>their companions); **Jer.** 9:4 (x2 – people, one of them); **Ezek.** 38:21 (>fellow); **Hag.** 2:22 (>comrade)

D. Changes Made to Avoid the Word "Man"

12. Removing "man" when the original Hebrew means "a male human being" (*'ish, gibbor, zaqar, bahur,* and also *'adam* [but only when *'adam* refers to a specific male person]) (247 inaccuracies)

Comment: Several Hebrew words that mean "man" and not "person" (unless they appear in certain recognized idioms) are changed and made gender-neutral. This is not because the meanings of these male-oriented Hebrew words have changed (the meanings have been known for centuries), but because the TNIV found these male-oriented words offensive to our modern culture, so it eliminated the most accurate translation "man" and substituted various other gender-neutral words. In each case this makes the translation less accurate because it eliminates male-specific meaning that is there in the Hebrew text.

It is especially difficult to understand cases like Deut. 21:15 (below). Why should the TNIV refuse to say that a person who "has two wives" is a *man*? Or in 1 Kings 9:5, what can be the objection to letting readers know that God promised David that his descendants would never lack a *man* on the throne of Israel?

Also troubling is Proverbs 27:17, a verse that is used as a theme verse for so many men's ministries: "As iron sharpens iron, so one man sharpens another." But the TNIV removes the men from this verse, even though the Hebrew word *'ish* clearly means "man"! With 3,686 male-oriented words expunged, the TNIV is not a Bible that will appeal to men, and this verse is an excellent example.

Examples:

Deuteronomy 21:15
NIV: If a <u>man</u> (*'ish*) has two wives, and he loves one but not the other...

TNIV: If <u>someone</u> has two wives, and he loves one but not the other...

1 Kings 9:5
NIV: I will establish your royal throne over Israel forever, as I promised David your father when I said, 'You shall never fail to have a <u>man</u> (*'ish*) on the throne of Israel.'

TNIV: I will establish your royal throne over Israel forever, as I promised David your father when I said, 'You shall never fail to have a <u>successor</u> on the throne of Israel.'

Proverbs 27:17
NIV: As iron sharpens iron, so one <u>man</u> (*'ish*) sharpens another.

TNIV: As iron sharpens iron, so one <u>person</u> sharpens another.

Isaiah 52:14 [Messianic passage]
NIV: Just as there were many who were appalled at him—his appearance was so disfigured beyond that of any <u>man</u> (*'ish*) and his form marred beyond human likeness—

TNIV: Just as there were many who were appalled at him—his appearance was so disfigured beyond that of any <u>human being</u> and his form marred beyond human likeness—

Complete List:
Gen. 2:5, 3:24, 25:27, 27:11; **Exod.** 11:7, 19:13, 21:20, 22:5; **Lev.** 16:21, 17:4, 25:26, 25:27, 25:29, 27:14, 27:16, 27:20, 27:28, 27:31; **Num.** 9:13 (x2), 16:17, 16:18, 17:9, 27:16; **Deut.** 11:25, 21:15, 21:18, 21:22, 27:15, 29:20, 33:8; **Josh.** 10:14; **Jdg.** 7:6, 7:7, 8:25, 16:19, 20:20, 20:22, 20:31; **1 Sam.** 1:21, 9:9, 11:8, 14:1, 14:24, 14:28, 26:2, 30:10 (x2); **2 Sam.** 16:7, 17:25, 20:1, 20:13; **1 Kgs.** 2:4, 7:14, 8:25, 9:5, 22:8; **2 Kgs.** 1:8, 7:5, 7:10, 9:4, 10:14, 18:21, 25:19; **1 Chron.** 26:12; **2 Chron.** 6:16, 7:18, 18:7, 23:7, 34:30; **Neh.** 5:13, 6:11, 7:2; **Ezra** 4:21 (Aramaic *gebar* "man"), 5:4 (Aramaic *gebar* "man"), 6:8 (Aramaic *gebar* "man"); **Job** 4:17, 10:5, 11:12, 14:10, 14:14, 15:16, 16:21 (x2), 22:2, 32:21, 33:29, 34:7, 34:9, 34:11, 34:21, 34:23, 34:30, 35:8, 37:20, 38:3, 38:26, 40:7; **Ps.** 1:1, 5:6, 18:48, 22:6, 25:12, 34:8, 37:23, 37:37, 38:14, 39:6, 39:11 (x2), 40:4, 43:1, 49:7, 49:16, 52:7, 62:3, 64:6, 88:4, 89:48, 94:12, 104:23, 112:1, 140:1, 140:4, 140:11; **Prov.** 3:31, 5:21, 10:23, 11:12, 11:17, 12:2, 12:8, 12:14, 12:25, 13:2, 13:8, 14:7, 14:12, 14:14, 14:17, 15:18, 15:21, 15:23, 16:2, 16:7, 16:14, 16:25, 16:28, 16:29, 17:27, 18:4, 18:12, 18:14, 18:20, 18:24, 19:6, 19:21, 19:22, 20:3, 20:5 (x2), 20:6, 20:17, 20:24, 21:2, 21:29, 22:29, 24:5 (x2), 24:29, 24:30 (*'adam* means "man" here because of *'ish* in 24:30a), 25:14, 25:18, 25:28, 26:12, 26:19, 26:21, 27:8, 27:17, 27:21, 28:11, 28:20, 28:21, 28:22, 29:1, 29:5, 29:6, 29:9, 29:20, 29:22, 29:23, 29:26; **Eccl.** 4:4, 6:2, 7:5, 11:9; **Isa.** 5:3, 5:7, 7:21, 31:3, 31:8, 32:2, 36:6, 44:13 (x2), 52:14 (man>human being, messianic context), 55:7, 66:3, 66:7; **Jer.** 9:12, 10:23 (x2), 13:11, 14:9, 17:5, 17:7, 17:10, 23:9, 23:36, 31:34 (x2), 32:32, 35:13, 35:19, 49:18, 49:33, 50:40, 51:43; **Lam.** 3:1, 3:27, 3:35, 3:39 (*'adam* parallel to *geber*); **Ezek.** 14:8, 18:8, 22:30, 28:2; **Dan.** 10:19; **Hos.** 6:9, 9:7; **Amos** 2:11; **Mic.** 2:2 (x2), 5:7, 6:8, 7:6; **Zech.** 4:1; **Mal.** 2:12

12a. The Hebrew nouns *gibbor* and *gibborim* when previously translated "mighty man/men" (21 inaccuracies)

Comment: The Hebrew noun *gibbor* means "strong, valiant man" (Brown-Driver-Briggs, *Hebrew and English Lexicon of the Old Testament*, p. 150; the word is related to the adjective *gibbor* which means "strong, mighty"). At least since the King James Version of the Bible (1611), the term *gibbor* has been translated as "mighty men" when referring to King David's elite circle of "thirty mighty men" and then his even greater "three mighty men" (especially in 2 Sam. 23 and 1 Chron. 11). The NIV had translated this word correctly as "mighty men" in these contexts, indicating both the strength of these men and their manhood. Surely in that ancient culture there were no women among David's thirty "mighty men"! It is hard to understand then why the TNIV changes and calls them "mighty warriors." But it is consistent with the TNIV pattern of removing male-oriented words from the text.

In an age when books are being written about the way men are staying away from church, it is ironic that the TNIV removes David's "mighty men." What man who reads about David's mighty men has not wanted to imitate their courage, their strength against evil, their faithfulness to God in serving their king? But in the TNIV they are no longer men! The TNIV is not a Bible that will appeal to men.

Examples:

<u>2 Samuel 23:8</u>
NIV: These are the names of David's <u>mighty men</u>: Josheb-Basshebeth, a Tahkemonite, was chief of the Three; he

raised his spear against eight hundred men, whom he killed in one encounter.

TNIV: These are the names of David's <u>mighty warriors</u>: Josheb-Basshebeth, a Tahkemonite, was chief of the Three; he raised his spear against eight hundred men, · whom he killed in one encounter.

Complete List:
("mighty men" > "mighty warriors" unless indicated otherwise) **2 Sam.** 23:8, 23:9, 23:16, 23:17, 23:22, **1 Chron.** 11:10, 11:11, 11:12, 11:19, 11:24, 11:26, 12:4, 27:6, 28:1 (x2, including "*gibbor* of strength"), 29:24, **Ps.** 52:1 (mighty man> mighty hero), 78:65 (mighty man>mighty warrior), **Isa.** 42:13 (mighty man>mighty champion), **Zech.** 10:5, 10:7

13. Removing mentions of the manhood of certain specific men   (9 inaccuracies)

Comment: These verses are different from category 12 in that the Hebrew terms used (such as *'enosh* or the plural *'anashim*) may not always mean "man" or "men," but they sometimes have that meaning, such as in these verses where the context shows that a specific man or only male human beings are in view. The 1984 NIV had the words "man" or "men" used accurately in these verses, but the TNIV has removed the word "man" even to refer to these specific individual men.

Examples:

Psalm 55:13 (A maskil of David)
NIV: But it is you, a <u>man</u> (*'enosh*) like myself, my companion, my close friend,

TNIV: But it is you, <u>one</u> like myself, my companion, my close friend,

Complete List:
Josh. 2:5; **Jdg.** 8:15; **2 Sam.** 2:14, 2:21, 4:2; **Ezra** 6:8; **Ps.** 55:13; **Jer.** 51:14; **Ezek.** 28:9

14. Removing "man" when it means "the human race" in the early parts of Genesis (20 inaccuracies)

Comment: God's activity of naming is important in the Bible. In Genesis 5:2 God names the human race "man" (*'adam*). That is the best translation because in the previous four chapters this same singular Hebrew word *'adam* has been used eight times to refer to man in distinction from woman (as in "The man and his wife were both naked, and they felt no shame," Gen. 2:25), and also five times as the proper name "Adam." So Hebrew readers would hear clear male nuances when God named the human race *'adam* in Genesis 5:2, and "man" is the best English translation. The TNIV incorrectly translates this word "human beings," which removes the male-oriented aspect of the name God gave the human race and also obscures the unity of the race that is suggested by the singular term "man" (and the Hebrew singular *'adam*). In this way the TNIV has renamed the human race with a gender-neutral term that is unlike the male-specific name God gave to it.

Beyond the context of the early chapters of Genesis the male nuance of *'adam* is not as clear, so we have not included in this list over 180 other verses where *'adam* refers to the whole human race or a significant or representative part of it. In many of these verses we would probably prefer the translation "man" (as it reflects this naming activity in Gen. 5:2 and retains a singular that reflects the unity of the race), but we can see that other translations might also be thought legitimate because the verses use *'adam* and not *'ish*, so we have not categorized them as translation inaccuracies. (We have included these verses in a separate paragraph following this section.)

Examples:

Genesis 1:26
NIV: So God created <u>man</u> in his own image, in the image of God he created him; male and female he created them.

TNIV: So God created <u>human beings</u> in his own image, in the image of God he created them; male and female he created them.

Genesis 5:2
NIV: He created them male and female and blessed them. And when they were created, he called them "<u>man</u>."(*'adam*)

TNIV: He created them male and female and blessed them. And when they were created, he called them "<u>human beings</u>."

Genesis 9:6
NIV: Whoever sheds the blood of <u>man</u>, by <u>man</u> shall his blood be shed; for in the image of God has God made

man.

TNIV: Whoever sheds <u>human</u> blood, by <u>human beings</u> shall their blood be shed; for in the image of God has God made <u>humankind</u>.

Complete List:
Gen. 1:26 (human beings), 1:27 (human beings), 5:1 (human beings), 5:2 (human beings), 6:1 (men>human beings), 6:2 (men>removed), 6:3 (human beings), 6:4 (men>human beings), 6:5 (human race), 6:6 (human beings), 6:7 (x2 – mankind>human race, men>with them), 7:21 (mankind>human race), 7:23, 8:21 (human beings),19:5, 9:6 (x3) 7

Additional note: Category 14.01: not counted as "inaccuracies": Also of interest is another category of changes (not counted in this list) in verses that use the singular noun *'adam* to speak of the whole human race, or part of the human race, or something characteristic of the human race. These are places that have been traditionally translated "man," and we would prefer the translation "man" here, but we recognize that *'adam* is not as male-specific as *'ish*. In addition, because these verses are distant from any contextual connection to the male-specific uses of *'adam* in the early chapters of Genesis, many of these verses could legitimately be translated "the person" or "one" so we have not counted these as translation "inaccuracies." In a number of cases the TNIV has also changed these to plurals, or has used "human" or "people" or some similar expression (cf. Brown-Driver-Briggs, *Hebrew and English Lexicon of the Old Testament* s.v. *'adam*, meaning 2): (183 examples, but not counted in this list of inaccuracies.)

Examples:

Proverbs 3:4
NIV: Then you will win favor and a good name in the sight of God and <u>man</u>.

TNIV: Then you will win favor and a good name in the sight of God and <u>humankind</u>.

Complete List:
Exod. 4:11, 8:17, 8:18, 9:9, 9:10, 9:19, 9:22, 9:25, 12:12, 13:2, 13:15, 30:32, **Lev.** 24:21, 27:28, **Deut.** 4:32, 5:24, **1 Sam.** 16:7 (x2), 26:19, **2 Sam.** 7:19, 23:3, 24:14, **1 Kgs.** 5:11, **2 Kgs.** 7:10, 19:18, **1 Chron.** 21:13, 29:1, **2 Chron.** 6:18, 19:6, 32:19, **Neh.** 2:12, **Job** 5:7, 7:20, 11:12, 14:1, 14:10, 20:4, 21:4, 21:33, 28:28, 31:33, 33:17, 33:23, 34:11, 34:15 (removed), 34:29, 36:25, 36:28, 37:7, **Ps.** 22:6, 36:6, 39:5, 39:11, 49:12, 49:20, 56:11, 58:11, 60:11, 64:9, 68:18, 76:10, 94:10, 94:11, 104:14, 104:23, 108:12, 115:4, 118:6, 118:8, 119:134, 124:2, 135:15, 144:3, 144:4, **Prov.** 3:4, 3:13, 8:34, 12:3, 16:1, 16:9, 17:18, 19:3, 19:11, 19:22, 20:25 (removed), 20:27, 21:16, 24:9, 24:30, 27:19 (x2), 27:20, 28:12, 28:17, 28:23, 29:23, 29:25, 30:2, 30:14, **Ecc.** 1:3, 2:21, 2:22, 2:24, 2:26, 3:19, 3:22, 5:18, 6:7, 6:10, 6:12, 7:2, 7:14, 7:20, 7:29, 8:6, 8:8, 8:15, 8:17, 9:1, 9:12, 11:8, 12:5, 12:13, **Isa.** 2:9, 2:17, 2:20, 2:22, 5:15, 13:12, 17:7, 29:21, 31:3, 43:4, 44:15 (removed), 58:5, **Jer.** 7:20, 9:21 (removed), 16:20, 17:5, 21:6, 31:27, 32:19, 32:20, 32:43, 33:5, 33:10, 33:12, 36:29, 45:12, 49:15, 50:3, 51:14, 51:62, **Lam.** 3:36, 3:39 (removed), **Ezek.** 14:7, 14:19, 19:3, 19:6, 20:11, 20:13, 20:21, 25:13, 29:8, 29:11, 32:13, 36:13, 36:14, **Amos** 4:13, **Jon.** 3:7, 3:8, **Hab.** 1:14, 2:8, 2:17, **Zeph** 1:3 (x2), **Hag.** 1:11, **Zech.** 2:8, 8:10 (x2), 9:1, 12:1, **Mal.** 3:8

14a. Hebrew *'enosh* meaning "man" when referring to the human race or a representative part of it, changed to "mortals" (11 inaccuracies)

Comment: The term *'enosh* could mean "man, mankind" (Brown-Driver-Briggs, *Hebrew and English Lexicon of the Old Testament*, p. 60) or perhaps "person, human being" (with no male connotation) depending on the context. But several times the TNIV has used the translation "mortal/mortals," which we count as inaccurate because it wrongly places a focus on mortality or liability to death, and this is not the meaning of the Hebrew word and is not true of man as originally created by God.

Examples:

Psalm 8:4
NIV: what is <u>man</u> that you are mindful of him, the son of man that you care for him?

TNIV: what are <u>mere mortals</u> that you are mindful of them, human beings that you care for them?

Psalm 103:15
NIV: As for <u>man</u>, his days are like grass, he flourishes like a flower of the field;

TNIV: As for <u>mortals</u>, their days are like grass, they flourish like a flower of the field;

Complete List:
2 Chron. 14:11 (mere mortals); **Job** 7:1 (mortals), 15:14 (mortals), 33:12 (any mortal), 36:25 (mortals); **Ps.** 8:4 (man>mere mortals), 9:19 (mortals), 9:20 (mortals), 10:18

(mere earthly mortals), 103:15 (mortals); **Isa.** 51:12 (mortal men>mere mortals)

14b. Hebrew *bene-'adam* (literally "children of man" but often "mankind" or "men" in the NIV) changed to something which removes man or men. (28 inaccuracies)

Examples:

Deuteronomy 32:8
NIV: When the Most High gave the nations their inheritance, when he divided all mankind, he set up boundaries for the peoples according to the number of the sons of Israel.

TNIV: When the Most High gave the nations their inheritance, when he divided all the human race, he set up boundaries for the peoples according to the number of the sons of Israel.

Proverbs 8:4
NIV: To you, O men, I call out; I raise my voice to all mankind.

TNIV: To you, O people, I call out; I raise my voice to all humankind.

Complete List:
Gen. 11:5 (the men>they); **Deut.** 32:8 (human race); **2 Chron.** 6:30 (human); **Ps.** 12:1 (men>human race, 12:8 (men>human race), 21:11 (mankind>human race), 31:20 (men>all), 33:13 (mankind>humankind), 66:5 (human-

kind), 89:47 (men>humanity), 90:3 (men>people), 107:15 (men> humankind), 107:21 (men>humankind), 107:31 (men>humankind), 115:16 (humankind), 145:12 (men> people); **Prov.** 8:4 (mankind>humankind), 8:31 (mankind>humankind); **Eccl.** 1:13 (men>human race), 2:3 (men>people), 3:10 (men> human race), 3:18 (men> human beings), 3:19 (x2 – human beings; humans), 3:21 (human), 9:3 (men>people); **Ezek.** 31:14 (mortal men> mortals); **Mic.** 5:7 (mankind>human being)

15. Removing comparisons between God and a man (4 inaccuracies)

Comment: Since the Bible often speaks of God in male-oriented terms such as "Father" and "King," it is not surprising that in comparisons the Bible sometimes says that God does something "like a man" or that he is not "like a man," using the male-specific term *'ish*. But these comparisons to a man have been removed by the TNIV. Why is there an objection to saying that God is like a man, or unlike a man, if that is what the Hebrew text means?

Examples:

Exodus 33:11

NIV: The LORD would speak to Moses face to face, as a man (*'ish*) speaks with his friend. Then Moses would return to the camp, but his young aide Joshua son of Nun did not leave the tent.

TNIV: The LORD would speak to Moses face to face, as one speaks to a friend. Then Moses would return to the camp, but his young aide Joshua son of Nun did not leave the tent.

Numbers 23:19
NIV: God is not a <u>man</u> (*'ish*), that he should lie, nor a son of man, that he should change his mind. Does he speak and then not act? Does he promise and not fulfill?

TNIV: God is not a <u>human</u>, that he should lie, not a human being, that he should change his mind. Does he speak and then not act? Does he promise and not fulfill?

Complete List:
Exod. 33:11 (*'ish*); **Num.** 23:19 (*'ish*); **Job** 9:32 (*'ish*); **Hos.** 11:9 (*'ish*)

16. Renaming occupations generally held by men in ancient Israel (33 inaccuracies)

Comment: In the verses below, designations of occupations have been changed to gender-neutral terms even in cases where the context or activity indicates that men were in view. These changes follow the general TNIV pattern of eliminating much of the male-oriented language in the Bible.

Examples:

Genesis 13:7
NIV: And quarreling arose between Abram's <u>herdsmen</u> and the <u>herdsmen</u> of Lot. The Canaanites and Perizzites were also living in the land at that time.

TNIV: And quarreling arose between Abram's <u>herders</u> and the <u>herders</u> of Lot. The Canaanites and Perizzites were also living in the land at that time.

Complete List:
Gen. 13:7 (x2 – herdsmen > herders), 13:8 (herdsmen > herders), 26:20 (x2 – herdsmen > herders; herdsmen... Isaac's herdsmen > herders...those of Isaac); **Exod.** 5:6 (foremen > overseers), 5:10 (foremen > overseers), 5:14 (foremen > overseers), 5:15 (foremen > overseers), 5:19 (foremen > overseers); **Deut.** 27:15 (craftsmen > skilled hands); **1 Kgs.** 5:18 (craftsmen > skilled workers), 7:14 (craftsman > skilled worker); **2 Kgs.** 24:14 (craftsmen > skilled workers), 24:16 (craftsmen > skilled workers); **1 Chron.** 4:14 (craftsmen > skilled workers), 29:5 (craftsmen > skilled workers); **2 Chron.** 2:14 (craftsmen > skilled workers); **Neh.** 4:22 (workmen > workers); **Isa.** 3:3(craftsmen > skilled workers), 19:8 (fishermen>those who fish), 40:19 (craftsman>metal worker), 40:20 (craftsman>skilled worker), 41:7 (craftsmen > skilled workers), 44:11 (craftsmen > skilled workers); **Jer.** 10:3 (craftsman > skilled worker), 10:9 (craftsman > engraver), 24:1 (craftsmen > skilled workers), 29:2 (craftsmen > skilled workers), 52:15 (craftsmen > skilled workers); **Ezek.** 47:10 (fishermen>those who fish); **Hos.** 8:6 (craftsman > metalworker), 13:2 (craftsmen > skilled hands)

17. Hebrew *'anashim* **(which can mean either "people" or "men" depending on context) where the context indicates that only men were in view. (11 inaccuracies)**

Examples:

<u>Joshua 10:18</u>
NIV: he said, "Roll large rocks up to the mouth of the cave, and post some <u>men</u> there to guard it.

TNIV: he said, "Roll large rocks up to the mouth of the cave, and post some <u>guards</u> there.

<u>Joshua 18:9</u>
NIV: So the <u>men</u> left and went through the land. They wrote its description on a scroll, town by town, in seven parts, and returned to Joshua in the camp at Shiloh.

TNIV: So <u>they</u> left and went through the land. They wrote its description on a scroll, town by town, in seven parts, and returned to Joshua in the camp at Shiloh.

Complete List:
Josh. 10:18, 18:9; **Jdg.** 9:28, 9:57, 20:12; **1 Sam.** 17:26; **1 Kings** 1:9; **2 Chron.** 34:12; **Neh.** 2:12, 13:25; **Zech.** 3:8

E. Changes Made to Avoid the Word "Son"

18. Removing "son of man" (6 inaccuracies)

Comment: The Hebrew word *ben* (singular) means "son," not "person" or "child." But in a number of cases the TNIV has translated it with a gender-neutral expression rather than using the most accurate translation, "son," which apparently was unacceptable because it was male-oriented. With the expression "son of man" this is particularly troubling because the expression is used so often by Jesus to speak of himself. This inappropriate TNIV change to Psalm 8:4 is also made in the New Testament when the verse is quoted in Hebrews 2:6 with a subsequent Messianic application to Jesus.

Examples:

Psalm 8:4
NIV: what is man that you are mindful of him, the <u>son of man</u> that you care for him?

TNIV: what are mere mortals that you are mindful of them, <u>human beings</u> that you care for them?

Numbers 23:19
NIV: God is not a man, that he should lie, nor a <u>son of man</u>, that he should change his mind. Does he speak and then not act? Does he promise and not fulfill?

TNIV: God is not a human, that he should lie, not a <u>human being</u>, that he should change his mind. Does he speak and then not act? Does he promise and not fulfill?

Job 25:6

NIV: how much less man, who is but a maggot—a <u>son of man</u>, who is only a worm!

TNIV: how much less a mortal, who is but a maggot—a <u>human being</u>, who is only a worm!

Complete List:

Num. 23:19; **Job** 25:6 ["son of man" > "human being"], 35:8 ["sons of men" > "member of the human race" (Heb. is singular *ben-'adam*)]; **Ps.** 8:4 ["son of man" > "human beings"]; 144:3 ["son of man" (*ben-'enosh* in Heb.) > "mortals"]; **Isa.** 51:12 ["sons of men" > "human beings" (Heb. is singular *ben-'adam*)]

19. Changing singular *ben* ("son") to "child" or "children" (19 inaccuracies)

Comment: These are inaccurate changes because in Hebrew *ben* (singular) always means "son," not "child," and certainly not "children" (plural). The TNIV again follows a pattern of not allowing English readers to know that the Bible uses an example of a specific male child to teach a general truth in verses like this (as in Deut. 6:20 or Prov. 13:24, below). In such verses, instead of letting readers know what the verse actually says, the TNIV has inaccurately translated the singular word that means "son" with a gender-neutral plural word such as "children."

   Some people today might not like it that the Bible frequently uses a male example to teach a general truth, but we should still continue to translate what the Bible actually does say, not change it to something that some people might like it to say.

Examples:

<u>Deuteronomy 6:20</u>
NIV: In the future, when your <u>son</u> asks you, "What is the meaning of the stipulations, decrees and laws the LORD our God has commanded you?" …

TNIV: In the future, when your <u>children</u> ask you, "What is the meaning of the stipulations, decrees and laws the LORD our God has commanded you?"…

<u>Proverbs 13:24</u>
NIV: He who spares the rod hates his <u>son</u>, but he who loves him is careful to discipline him.

TNIV: Those who spare the rod hate their <u>children</u>, but those who love them are careful to discipline them.

Complete List:
Exod. 13:14 ; **Deut.** 6:20, 7:4 ; **Prov.** 10:1 (x2), 13:1, 13:24, 15:20, 17:25, 19:13, 19:18, 19:26, 19:27, 27:11, 28:7, 29:17; **Eccl.** 5:14; **Ezek.** 18:4, 18:202

F. Changes Made to Avoid the Word "Women"

20. Changing "women" to "weaklings" (4 inaccuracies)

Comment: Some Old Testament verses show judgment or shame on a nation when its soldiers are women or have become "like women." Several writers have appealed to these verses in recent years to argue that women should not serve in combat functions in our military forces, for the Bible views it as shameful and a mark of disgrace to a nation – it is the responsibility of the men of a nation to bear the burden of protecting it in time of war.

In each of these four verses the Hebrew word is *nashim*, the plural of *'ishshah* and the ordinary, common word for "women" (it is not a rare word, and there is no debate or uncertainty over its meaning, for *'ishshah* occurs 847 times in the Old Testament).

But in these verses related to military combat, the TNIV has removed the correct translation "women" and replaced it with "weaklings." The word does not mean that. Perhaps some people think that is what these verses *imply*, but that is not what they say. Perhaps the verses also suggest shame that any people would allow their women to serve in combat, or shame that all the men have been defeated and only women are left to defend a nation. In any case, the point is that even the original Hebrew readers would have had to ponder for a moment what the verse meant when it said the troops had become women (or in some verses had become "like women"). It is not proper translation to hide from the English readers the fact that the Bible said in these verses that some troops had become women or had become "like women."

The TNIV is a "gender-neutral" version because it eliminates so many gender-specific words from the Bible when they accurately represent the original text, mostly male-specific terms but in this case female-specific terms as well.

Examples:

Nahum 3:13 (judgment against Nineveh)
NIV: Look at your troops-- they are all <u>women</u>! The gates of your land are wide open to your enemies; fire has consumed their bars.

TNIV: Look at your troops-- they are all <u>weaklings</u>. The gates of your land are wide open to your enemies; fire has consumed the bars of your gates.

Isaiah 19:16
NIV: In that day the Egyptians will be like <u>women</u>. They will shudder with fear at the uplifted hand that the LORD Almighty raises against them.

TNIV: In that day the Egyptians will become <u>weaklings</u>. They will shudder with fear at the uplifted hand that the LORD Almighty raises against them.

Complete List:
Isa. 19:16 (against Egypt), **Jer.** 50:37 (against Babylon), **Jer.** 51:30 (against Babylon), **Nah.** 3:13 (against Nineveh)

Translation Inaccuracies
in the 2005 TNIV New Testament:
An Updated Categorized List of 910 Examples

Note: This list of translation inaccuracies, which was originally based on the 2002 *Today's New International Version – New Testament*, has now been updated to correspond to the revised New Testament in the 2005 TNIV. We found that some inaccuracies in the 2002 TNIV have been corrected by the translation committee and others have been introduced, with the result that this list has been changed from 901 examples to 910 examples.

All the changes noted here are from the 1984 NIV (which had translated gender language accurately in these verses) to the 2005 TNIV.

Most of the changes in this list have to do with gender language, and the changes have been made to avoid using five words with masculine meaning or nuance: father, brother, son, man, and he/him/his. However, at the end we have also included a list of 24 verses that were changed to avoid using the phrase "the Jews" and 41 verses where the nuance of holiness in "saints" has been lost.

With regard to the use of gender language, it seems to us that in every case listed here the change eliminates masculine meaning or masculine nuances that are present in the underlying Greek terms, and also that these changes frequently go beyond the legitimate bounds of ordinary, well-established meanings for the common Greek words being translated (though in some cases there are differences among the lexicons, as noted in the individual categories below). These examples therefore seem to us to be "translation inaccuracies" that were included in the TNIV for the sake of producing a more "gender neutral" or "inclusive language" version.

This list was prepared under general oversight of The Council on Biblical Manhood and Womanhood, and has been compared for accuracy against the Greek New Testament. In the event that readers may find any corrections or additions that may need to be made, we would welcome your input sent to us at: office@cbmw.org

A. Changes from Singular to Plural to Avoid the Use of "He/Him/His"

"he/him/his/himself" changed to *"they/them/their /themselves"* **(where Greek has singular verb and/or masculine singular 3rd person pronoun) (217)**

Matt. 10:10, 24 (2x), 25 (2x), 38, 39 (2x); 12:35 (2x); 13:12 (3x), 19, 21 (3x), 23, 57 (2x); 16:24, 25 (2x); 18:15 (2x), 17 (2x); 23:12 (2x); 25:29 (3x); **Mark** 2:22 (2x); 4:25 (2x); 6:4 (3x); 8:34 (2x), 35 (2x); 13:13; **Luke** 4:24; 5:37; 6:40 (2x), 45 (2x), 47, 48; 8:18 (3x); 9:24 (2x); 10:7; 12:21; 14:11 (2x); 14:27; 16:16; 17:33 (2x); 18:14 (2x); 19:26; **John** 3:20 (2x), 21; 4:14 (3x), 36 (2x), 44; 7:53; 11:9, 10 (2x); 12:25 (2x), 35, 45 (2x), 47, 48; 13:10 (2x), 16 (2x); 14:12; 15:15, 20; 16:2; **Rom.** 4:8; 14:4 (4x), 6, 22, 23 (2x); 15:2; **1 Cor.** 4:5; 6:18 (2x); 8:2 (2x); 11:29; 14:2 (2x), 4, 5, 13 (2x), 16, 28 (2x), 37, 38; **2 Cor.** 9:9 (3x); 10:18; 11:20; **Gal.** 4:1 (2x), 2 (2x); 6:6, 7, 8; **Eph.** 4:28 (2x); 5:29 (3x); **Phil.** 3:4; **Col.** 2:18 (3x), 19; 3:25; **2 Thess.** 3:14 (2x), 15 (2x); **1 Tim.** 5:18; **2 Tim.** 2:21; **Titus** 3:10 (2x), 11; **Heb.** 2:6 (2x), 7 (2x), 8 (4x); 4:10; **Jas.** 1:7, 8, 9, 10 (2x), 11 (2x), 12 (2x), 23, 24 (2x), 25 (3x), 26 (4x); 2:14, 24; 5:19; **2 Pet.** 2:19; **1 John** 2:4, 5, 10

(2x), 11 (3x); 3:3, 9 (3x), 10; 5:16, 18 (2x); **Rev.** 2:27, 28; 3:5 (2x), 12 (3x); 16:15 (2x); 21:7 (2x)

"he/him/his/himself" (with singular Greek verb and/or masculine 3rd person singular Greek pronoun) changed to *"they/them/their/themselves"* (with singular antecedent in English; these are examples of the so-called "singular they") **(159)**

Matt. 5:39, 41; 10:38, 39 (2x); 11:15; 13:9, 43; 15:4, 5, 6 (2x); 16:24 (2x), 25 (2x), 27; 18:6 (3x), 15 (2x), 16, 17 (3x); 24:18; **Mark** 2:21; 4:9, 23; 7:10, 11, 12 (2x); 8:34 (2x), 35 (2x); 9:42 (3x); 11:25; 13:16; **Luke** 2:3; 5:36 (2x); 8:8, 16; 9:23 (2x), 24 (2x); 14:27, 35; 17:3 (3x), 4 (2x), 33 (2x); **John** 3:4 (3x), 18, 36; 6:40, 44, 65 (2x); 7:18, 38; 10:9; 11:25; 14:21 (3x), 23 (3x); **Acts** 2:6; 4:32 (2x); 25:16 (3x); **Rom.** 2:6; 4:4 (2x), 5; 8:9, 24; 11:35 ("who"?); 14:2, 5; **1 Cor.** 3:8 (2x); 8:10; 11:28 (2x), 29 (2x); 10:24; 14:24, 25 (2x); **2 Cor.** 5:10; 10:7 (3x); **1 Tim.** 5:8 (2x); 6:4 (2x); **2 Tim.** 2:4; **Jas.** 3:13 (2x); 4:11; 5:13 (2x), 14 (3x), 15 (4x), 20 (2x); **1 John** 2:5; 3:15, 17; 4:15 (2x), 16; **2 John** 1:10 (2x), 11 (2x); **Rev.** 2:7, 11, 17, 29; 3:6, 12, 13, 20 (2x), 22; 13:9, 10 (2x); 14:9 (2x), 10 (2x); 22:12

"he/him/his/himself" (singular verb and/or masculine singular 3rd person pronoun in Greek) changed to *"those"* (often *"those who"*) **(36)**

Matt. 7:8 (2x), 21; 10:22; **Luke** 6:47; 11:10 (2x); **John** 15:23; **Rom.** 14:1, 6 (3x); **1 Cor.** 1:31; 7:22 (2x); 14:4 (2x), 5, 38; **2 Cor.** 10:17; **Eph.** 4:28; **2 Thess.** 3:14; **1 Pet.** 4:1; **Rev.** 2:7, 11, 17, 26; 3:5, 12, 21; 22:7, 11 (4x), 17

"he/him/his/himself" changed to "*you/your/yourself*" (90)

Matt. 6:24 (2x); 6:27; 7:9; 10:36; 16:26 (4x); **Mark** 7:15 (3x), 18, 19 (3x), 20; 8:36, 37, 38; 11:23 (3x); **Luke** 5:39; 9:25, 26; 11:8 (4x); 12:25; 13:15; 14:28 (2x), 29 (2x), 33; 16:13 (2x); **John** 15:5 (2x), 6; 16:32; **1 Cor.** 3:18 (3x); 6:1; 7:17 (2x), 20 (2x), 24; 16:2; **2 Cor.** 9:7 (2x); **Gal.** 6:3 (4x), 4 (4x), 5; **Eph.** 4:25; 6:8 (2x); **1 Thess.** 4:4; **Jas.** 1:5 (2x), 6 (2x), 14 (2x); 4:17; **1 Pet.** 3:10 (2x), 11 (2x); **2 Pet.** 1:9 (3x); **1 John** 2:15; 3:17; 5:16 (2x); **Rev.** 22:18, 19 (2x)

"he/him/his/himself" changed to "*we/our/ourselves*" (9)

Rom. 14:7 (2x—ourselves); 12 (ourselves); 15:2 (ourselves); **1 John** 4:20 (5x--we)

"he/him/his/himself" changed to *no pronoun* (sentence changed to other wording) (17 verses)

Matt. 5:22; 18:4; **Luke** 6:45; 9:62; 12:8, 15, 47 (2x); 14:26; **John** 7:18; **1 Thess.** 4:6; **1 John** 2:9, 11; 3:15, 17; 4:20; 5:10

"he/him/his/himself" is *omitted* (25)

Matt. 5:40; 10:32, 33, 42; 12:29 (2x); 18:15; **Mark** 8:34; 9:35, 41; 10:28; 13:34; **Luke** 9:48; 10:6; 11:8; **John** 3:27; 7:17; **1 Cor.** 2:14; **1 Thess.** 4:6;   **2 Tim.** 2:5, 21; **Heb.** 10:38; **Jas.** 4:11; 5:13, 14;

"he/him/his/himself" changed to "*other*" (2)

Matt. 18:15 (omit "your" and "you"); **1 John** 5:16 (any)

"whoever" (singular) changed to *"those" (often "those who")* (12)

Matt. 13:12 (2x); 23:12 (2x); **Mark** 4:25 (2x); **Luke** 8:18 (2x); **John** 3:21; 4:14; **1 John** 2:11; **Rev.** 22:17

"anyone" (singular) changed to *"those" (often "those who")* (6)

John 16:2; **1 Cor.** 14:2; **James** 1:23; 3:2; **1 John** 3:10; **Rev.** 13:18

"one" (singular) changed to *"those" (often "those who")* (8)

Luke 6:49; **John** 12:48; **1 Cor.** 14:5; **2 Cor.** 10:18 (2x); **Gal.** 6:8 (2x); **1 John** 3:9

"everyone" (singular) changed to *"those" (often "those who")* (7)

Matt. 25:29 (2x); **Luke** 14:11 (2x); 18:14; **John** 3:20; **1 Cor.** 14:3

Other changes from singular to plural for the whole sentence (20)

Matt. 10:10, 24 (2x); 13:19, 20, 57; 19:23, 24; **Mark** 2:22; **John** 11:9, 10; 12:25 (2X), 35, 44, 47; 13:10; **Rom.** 13:4;

14:23; **Gal.** 4:7; **2 Tim.** 2:21; **1 John** 2:4; 3:10; **Rev.** 21:7; 22:7

Words left untranslated in process of changing verse from singular to plural or from masculine to gender-neutral (2)

Matt. 18:17 ("them"); **Heb.** 12:9 ("human")

B. Changes to Avoid the Word "Father" and Related Words

"father" (*pater*, singular) changed to "*parents*" (1)

Acts 7:20

"fathers" (*pater*, plural) changed to "*parents*" or "*people*" (2)

(Though "parents" is sometimes acceptable as a meaning for the plural of *pater*, in this case the context is speaking of fatherly discipline)

Acts 7:11; **Heb.** 12:9

"fathers"/forefathers" (*pater*, plural) changed to *ancestors* (34)

(The BDAG Lexicon, p. 786-787, gives "ancestors" as a possible meaning, but the LSJ Lexicon (p. 1348) only gives the meaning of "forefathers." We have included these verses in this list because they seem to us to fit the general pattern of excluding male nuances in the TNIV, and because the male nuance or connotation of the plural word *pateres* would have been evident to the original Greek readers, but "ancestors" has no evident relationship to the word "father" and no male connotation in English.)

Matt. 23:30, 32; **Luke**1:55, 72; 6:23, 26; 11:47, 48; **John** 4:20; 6:31, 49, 58; **Acts** 5:30; 7:12, 15, 19, 38, 39, 44, 45, 51, 52; 13:17, 32, 36; 15:10; 22:14; 26:6; 28:25; **1 Cor.** 10:1; **Heb.** 1:1; 3:9; 8:9; **2 Pet.** 3:4

C. Changes to Avoid the Word "Brother" (Or to Add the Word "Sister")

"brother" (*adelphos*, **singular**) **changed to** *"brother"* **or** *"sister"* **(19)**

Matt. 5:22 (2x), 23; 18:15, 35; **Luke** 17:3; **Rom.** 14:10 (2x), 13, 15, 21; **1 Cor.** 8:11, 13; **1 Thess.** 4:6; **Jas.** 4:11; **1 John** 3:10, 17; 4:20; 5:16

"brother" (*adelphos*, **singular**) **changed to** *"(fellow) believer"* **(5)**

(The BDAG Lexicon, p. 18, lists "brother, fellow member, member, associate" as possible meanings for *adelphos*, but all the singular examples listed refer to male human beings. The earlier BAGD Lexicon, p. 16, did not give these meanings, and the new BDAG Lexicon (2000) gives no new examples or new arguments to justify these new meanings that it proposes. The LSJ Lexicon (p. 20) gives the meaning "brother (as a fellow Christian)", but does not give the meaning "believer.")

2 Thess. 3:6; **1 John** 2:9, 11; 3:15; 4:20

"brother" (*adelphos,* **singular) changed to "***(fellow) believers***" (4)**

1 Cor. 5:11; **2 Thess.** 3:15; **Jas.** 1:9; **1 John** 2:10

"brother" (*adelphos,* **singular) changed to** *"other"* **(15)**

Matt. 5:24 (that person); 7:3 (someone else), 4 (omitted), 5 (other person); 18:15 (them), 21 (someone); **Luke** 6:41 (someone else), 42 (friend, other person); **1 Cor.** 8:13 (them); **1 Thess.** 4:9 ("brotherly love" to "your love for one another"); **Heb.** 8:11 (one another); **James** 4:11 (them); **2 Pet.** 1:7 (mutual affection--2x); **1 John** 4:21 (one another)

"brothers" (*adelphos,* **plural) changed to "***brothers and sisters***" (where sisters is uncertain or doubtful) (8)**

Acts 1:16; 2:29; 13:26, 38; **2 Cor.** 11:9; **Heb.** 2:17; **Jas.** 3:1; **Rev.** 19:10

"brothers/brotherhood" (*adelphos,* **plural) changed to** *"fellow believers"* **(4)**

Acts 15:22; **1 Tim.** 6:2; **1 Pet.** 2:17; 5:9

"brothers" (*adelphos,* **plural) changed to** *"believers"*

(27)

John 21:23; **Acts** 9:30; 10:23; 11:1, 29; 15:1, 3, 22, 32, 33, 36, 40; 16:2, 40; 17:6, 10, 14; 18:18, 27; 21:7, 17; 28:14, 15; **2 Cor.** 11:26; **Gal.** 2:4; **3 John** 1:3, 10

"brothers" (*adelphos*, plural) changed to *"other"* (11)

Matt. 5:47 (own people); 22:5 (associates); 28:21 (our people); **Acts** 22:5 ("associates"); 28:21 ("our people"); **1 Cor.** 8:12 (them); **1 Thess.** 4:10 (dear friends); 5:26 (God's people); **1 John** 3:14 (each other), 16 (one another); **Rev.** 22:9 (fellow prophets)

"brothers"(*adelphos*, plural) omitted (2)

Matt. 7:4; **1 Cor.** 15:31 (TNIV uses less likely variant reading)

D. Changes to Avoid the Word "Man"

"man" or "husband" (*aner*, singular) changed to "*other*" (7)

(The BDAG Lexicon (p. 79) gives as the general definition of *aner* the meaning, "a male person," and under that general definition it gives as meaning 2, "equivalent to *tis*, someone, a person." All the examples they list under meaning 2 either clearly refer to a male human being (as Luke 19:2, for example, "and there was a *man* named Zacchaeus"), or the context is not determinative but the meaning "man" makes good sense and the meaning "person" is not required. BDAG at the end of this entry also notes an idiom, *kat-andra*, which clearly means "man for man, individually," and clearly includes women in some instances, but that idiom does not occur in the New Testament. The LSJ Lexicon (p. 138) also notes the idiom *kat-andra*, with a similar meaning. The LSJ Lexicon does not give the meaning "person" for *aner*, but rather, "man, opposed to women," "man, opposed to god," "man, opposed to youth," "man emphatically, man indeed," "husband," and some special usages. For further discussion on the word *aner*, "man," see Vern Poythress and Wayne Grudem, *The Gender Neutral Bible Controversy* (Nashville: Broadman and Holman, 2000), p. 101, note 2, and pages 321-333; see also, "Can Greek *aner* ("man") sometimes mean "person"?" at www.cbmw.org/TNIV/aner.html.)

Rom. 4:8 (those); **1 Tim.** 3:2, 12 ("husband" to "faithful" on both); **Jas.** 1:12 (those), 20 (our), 23 (people); 2:2 (someone)

"man" (*aner*, singular) *omitted* **(2)**

Jas. 1:8; 3:2

"men" (*aner*, plural) changed to "*people*"(10)

Matt. 12:41; **Luke** 11:31, 32; **Acts** 2:22; 3:12; 13:16; 17:22, 34; 19:35; 21:28

"men" (*aner*, **plural**) **changed to** *"other"* **(4)**

Acts 14:15 (friends); 17:34 (people); 19:25 (friends); 20:30 (some)

"men" (*aner*, **plural**) *omitted* **(2)**

Luke 14:24; **Acts** 15:22 (Judas Barsabbas & Silas)

"man" (*anthropos*, **singular**) **changed to** *"people"* **or other plural nouns (9)**

Matt. 12:35 (2x); 18:7; **Luke** 6:45 (2x); **Rom.** 1:23; 4:6; **Gal.** 6:7; **2 Tim.** 3:17

"man" (*anthropos*, **singular**) **changed to** *"you/your"* **(10)**

Matt. 10:36; 15:11, 18, 20; 16:26 (2x); **Mark** 7:23; 8:36, 37; **Luke** 9:25

"man" (*anthropos*, **singular**) **changed to** *"human being/human/mere mortal"* **when referring to a specific historical man (6)**

Acts 10:26 (Peter); **Acts** 12:22 (Herod); **1 Cor.** 15:21 (Jesus); **Phil.** 2:8 (Jesus); **1 Tim.** 2:5 (Jesus); **Jas.** 5:17 (Elijah)

"men" (*anthropos*, **plural**) **changed to** *"people"* **when referring to male human beings (1)**

Heb. 5:1 (high priests)

"men" (*anthropos*, **plural) changed to** *"other"* **(8)**

(Neither the meaning "man" nor the meaning "person" is represented in these verses.)

Matt. 5:13 (underfoot); 10:32 (publicly), 33 (publicly); **Luke** 12:8 (publicly), 9 (publicly), 36 (servants); **John** 8:17 (witnesses); **1 Cor.** 7:7 (you)

"men" (*anthropos*, **singular or plural)** *omitted* **(8)**

Matt. 10:17; 16:26 (2x) 19:12; **Luke** 12:8; **Acts** 4:12 (no other name under heaven); 17:26 (all nations); **1 Tim.** 5:24 (sins of some)

"man" (*anthropos,* **singular) meaning the human race changed to** *"people/mortals/human"* **(6)**

Matt. 4:4; **Mark** 2:27 (2x); **Luke** 4:4; **John** 2:25; **Heb.** 2:6 (mere mortals); 13:6 (human beings)

E. Changes to Avoid the Word "Son"

"son" (*huios,,* **singular) changed to** *"child"* **(3)**

Matt. 23:15; **Luke** 14:5; **Heb.** 12:6

"son" (*huios,,* **singular) changed to** *"children"* **(3)**

Gal. 4:7 (2x—sentence plural); **Rev.** 21:7 (sentence plural)

"sons" (*huios*, plural) changed to *"children"* (16)

Matt. 5:9, 45; 17:25, 26; **Luke** 6:35; **John** 12:36; **Rom.** 8:14, 19; 9:26; **Gal.** 3:26; **1 Thess.** 5:5 (2x); **Heb.** 12:5, 7 (2x), 8

"sons" (*huios*, plural) changed to *"people"* (2)

Matt. 13:38 (2x)

"sons" (*huios*, plural) changed to *"sons and daughters"* (1)

Heb. 2:10

F. Changes to Avoid the Phrase "The Jews"

"the Jew(s)" (*hoi ioudaioi*) changed to *"Jewish leaders"* (15)

The 2000 BDAG Lexicon (pages 478-479) objects to translating *hoi ioudaioi* as "the Jews" because it claims that "many readers or auditors of Bible translations to not practice the historical judgment necessary to distinguish between circumstances and events of an ancient time and contemporary ethnic-religions-social realities, with the result that anti-Judaism in the modern sense of the term is needlessly fostered through biblical texts" (p. 478). In other words, we should no longer translate *hoi ioudaioi* as "the Jews" because many Bible readers today will not realize that the Bible is talking about ancient Judaism, not modern Judaism. So it favors the translation, "Judean."

However, we find this argument unpersuasive and believe that the term "Judean" will wrongly imply a reference to people who simply live in a certain geographical area, whether Jews or not, and will not adequately convey the religious and ethnic identification with the ancient Jewish people that the term "the Jews" implies.

On the next page, the BDAG Lexicon discusses the phrase *hoi ioudaioi* when it is used of people who are opposed to Jesus, and says the following: "Those who are in opposition to Jesus, with special focus on hostility emanating from leaders in Jerusalem, center of Israelite belief and cult; there is no indication that John uses the term in the general ethnic sense suggested in modern use of the word *Jew*, which covers diversities of belief and practice that were not envisaged by biblical writers …" (p. 479). In other words, John does not use the word "Jew" to speak of modern Judaism or anything like the diversity of modern Judaism.

The implication of this BDAG comment is, again, that modern readers will not understand that John is referring to ancient Jews in the first century and that these are different from modern Jews in the 21st century. While we agree that John did not use *hoi ioudaioi* to refer to modern Judaism, we believe that readers of the Bible are able to realize that they are reading about events that occurred in ancient history. To take another example, when Bible readers today read that "Jesus entered Peter's house" (Matt. 8:14), we don't avoid using the word "house" out of fear that people will think Matthew meant a modern house with electricity and air-conditioning and an automatic dishwasher. Readers automatically realize that they are reading an ancient document and that "house" refers to whatever kind of house people had in first century Palestine. Even if the BDAG Lexicon is correct in saying that *hoi ioudaioi* can be used "with special focus on hostility emanating from leaders in Jerusalem," that does not mean that *only* the leaders were involved in such opposition to Jesus, for no doubt many common people were involved as well. And there were some Jewish leaders, such as Nicodemus (see John 3) who did not join in the opposition to Jesus. So it seems to us that changing *hoi ioudaioi* from "the Jews" to "Jewish leaders" introduces an incorrect change of meaning into a translation.

The older BAGD Lexicon (1979) simply translates *hoi ioudaioi* as "the Jews" (p. 379). The LSJ Lexicon simply translates *ho ioudaios* (singular form) as "a Jew," and gives no special meaning for the plural form (p. 832).

John 1:19; 5:10, 15, 16; 7:1, 11, 13; 9:22; 18:14, 36; 19:31, 38; 20:19; **Acts** 13:50; 21:11

"the Jew(s)" (*hoi ioudaioi*) **changed to** *"they"* **or omitted (9)**

John 2:20; 5:18; 8:52, 57; 9:18, 22; 10:33; 18:31; **Acts** 18:14

G. Changes that Lose the Nuance of Holiness in "Saints"

"saints" (Greek *hagios*, plural) changed to "people" or "God's people" or "Lord's people" or "your people" (41)

Acts 9:13, 32; 26:10; **Rom.** 8:27; 15:25, 26, 31; 16:2, 15; **1**

Cor. 6:1, 2; 14:33; 16:15; **2 Cor.** 8:4; 9:1; 13:13; **Eph.** 1:15, 18; 2;19; 3:18; 6:18; **Phil.** 4:21, 22; **Col.** 1:4, 12, 26; **1 Tim.** 5:10**; Philem.** 1:5, 7; **Jude** 1:3; **Rev.** 5:8; 8:3, 4; 11:18; 13:7, 10; 16:6; 17:6; 18:20, 24; 19:8

H. Other Gender Related Changes

Other gender related changes (7)

Acts 12:13 ("girl" dropped); 19:24 ("craftsmen" to "workers"), 25 ("workmen" to "workers"), 38 ("craftsmen" to "associates"); **1 Cor.** 7:29 ("wives" to "are married"); **2 Cor.** 11:13 ("workmen" to "workers"); **1 Tim.** 2:12 ("have authority" to "assume authority")

Other examples of unnecessary removal of masculine references to God or Christ (5)

John 1:33 (the one who); 6:33 (that which; margin: he who); 10:2 (the one); **Heb.** 2:6 (the "son of man," apparent Messianic prophecy or theme that the author of Hebrews sees fulfilled in Christ, from Ps. 8:4, changed to "human beings"

Summary Chart of Translation Inaccuracies in the TNIV Old Testament by Category

Category		Inaccuracies	Singular to Plural
A. Changes made to remove "he/him/his"			
1	Changing 3rd person masculine singular to 3rd person plural	857	857
1a	Pluralizing 3rd person masculine singular pronouns involving Hebrew *nephesh*	18	18
1b	Changing other words from singular to plural	291	291
2	Changing "him" to "they" with a singular antecedent	474	474
2a	Pluralizing w/ singular English antecedent involving Hebrew *nephesh*	27	27
3	Changing the 3rd person singular pronoun to 2nd person	64	64
4	Changing the 3rd person singular pronoun to 1st person plural	8	8
5	Changing "whoever," "anyone," "everyone," "those/those who"	13	13
6	Removing the 3rd person masculine singular pronoun	255	255
7	Completely omitting words represented in Hebrew	13	
B. Changes made to remove "father"			
8	Changing singular *'ab* to "parent" or "parents"	19	
9	Changing plural *'aboth* to ancestors	287	
10	Diminishing the role of the father in ancient Israelite society	11	
C. Changes made to remove "brother"			

11	Changing "brother" to another word with no familial connotation	26	

D. Changes made to remove "man"

12	Removing "man" when the word means a male human being	247	
12a	Changing "mighty men" to "mighty warriors"	21	
13	Removing mentions of the manhood of certain historical men	9	
14	Removing man when it means the "human race" in Genesis	20	
14a	Hebrew 'enosh meaning man w/ reference to human race	11	
14b	Hebrew bene-'adam changed to remove "man" or "men"	28	
15	Removing comparisons between God and a man	4	
16	Renaming occupations generally held by men	33	
17	Hebrew 'anashim where context shows only men in view	11	

E. Changes made to remove "son"

18	Removing "son of man"	6	
19	Changing singular ben to "child" or "children"	19	19

F. Changes made to remove "women"

20	Changing "women" to "weaklings"	4	

Total singular to plural changes			**2,026**
Total translation inaccuracies TNIV Old Testament		**2,776**	
New Testament translation inaccuracies (second list)		**910**	
Total translation inaccuracies for whole TNIV		**3,686**	

[This list may be updated from time to time: see www.no-tniv.com or www.cbmw.org.]

Appendix 3:
Statements of Concern about the TNIV

A. Statement of Concern by Evangelical Leaders

We cannot endorse the TNIV as sufficiently trustworthy to commend to the church. We do not believe it is a translation suitable for use as a normal preaching and teaching text of the church or for a common memorizing, study, and reading Bible of the Christian community.

Hudson T. Armerding
President Emeritus
Wheaton College
Wheaton, Illinois

Ted Baehr
President & Founder
Christian Film & Television
Commission
Camarillo, California

Frank Barker
Pastor
Briarwood Presbyterian
Church
Birmingham, Alabama

Timothy B. Bayly
Pastor
Church of the Good Shepherd
Bloomington, Indiana

Alistair Begg
Pastor
Parkside Church
Chagrin Falls, Ohio

Tal Brooke
President & Chairman
Spiritual Counterfeits Project,
Inc.
Berkeley, California

Bryan Chapell
President
Covenant Seminary
St. Louis, Missouri

Charles Colson
Founder
Prison Fellowship Ministry
Washington, D.C.

Darryl DelHousaye
Pastor
Scottsdale Bible Church
Scottsdale, Arizona

Nancy Leigh DeMoss
Author & Radio Host
Revive Our Hearts Ministries
Niles, Michigan

James C. Dobson
Founder & Chairman
Focus on the Family
Colorado Springs, Colorado

Dan Doriani
Senior Pastor of Central Pres-
byterian Church &
Professor of New Testament
Covenant Theological
Seminary
St. Louis, MO

J. Ligon Duncan, III
Moderator of the General
Assembly of the Presbyterian
Church in America & Pastor
First Presbyterian Church
Jackson, Mississippi

Michael J. Easley
President
Moody Bible Institute
Chicago, Illinois

Stuart W. Epperson, Jr.
Chairman
Salem Communications
Corporation
Winston-Salem, North
Carolina

Steve Farrar
President
Men's Leadership Ministries
Frisco, Texas

Jerry Falwell
Founder & Chancellor
Liberty University
Lynchburg, Virginia

Sandy Finlayson
Director of Library Services
Westminster Theological
Seminary
Philadelphia, PA

Ronnie Floyd
Senior Pastor
First Baptist Church
Springdale, Arkansas

Jack Graham
Pastor
Prestonwood Baptist Church
Plano, TX

Wayne Grudem
Professor
Phoenix Seminary
Scottsdale, Arizona

Joshua Harris
Senior Pastor
Covenant Life Church
Gaithersburg, Maryland

Ken Hemphill
National Strategist
Empowering Kingdom
Growth
Southern Baptist Convention

Roland S. Hinz
President
HiTorque Publishing
Pasadena, California

H. Wayne House
Professor
Faith Seminary
Tacoma, WA

Susan Hunt
Women's Ministry Consultant
Presbyterian Church in
America
Marietta, Georgia

Rebecca Jones
Homemaker, Author, Editor
Escondido, California

Mary Kassian
Author & Speaker
Alabaster Flask Ministries
Alberta, Canada

Charles S. Kelley, Jr.
President
New Orleans Baptist
Theological Seminary
New Orleans, Louisiana

Rhonda H. Kelley
Professor of Women's
Ministry
New Orleans Baptist
Theological Seminary
New Orleans, Louisiana

D. James Kennedy
Chancellor
Knox Theological Seminary
Fort Lauderdale, Florida

Charles E. Klein
National Director
Student Venture
Escondido, California

Beverly J. LaHaye
Chairman
Concerned Women for
America

Tim F. LaHaye
Author, Minister, Educator

Robert Lewis
Pastor
Fellowship Bible Church
Little Rock, Arkansas

H. B. London
Vice President
Focus on the Family
Colorado Springs, Colorado

Erwin Lutzer
Senior Pastor
Moody Church
Chicago, Illinois

John MacArthur
President
Master's Seminary
Los Angeles, California

James MacDonald
Pastor
Harvest Bible Chapel
Rolling Meadows, Illinois

C. J. Mahaney
President
Sovereign Grace Ministries
Gaithersburg, Maryland

Tom Mason
Executive Vice President
Focus on the Family
Colorado Springs, Colorado

R. Albert Mohler, Jr.
President
The Southern Baptist
Theological Seminary
Louisville, Kentucky

Joel Nederhood
Director of Ministries
Emeritus
The Back to God Hour
Lansing, Illinois

Niel Nielson
President
Covenant College
Chattanooga, Tennessee

Marvin Olasky
Editor-in-Chief
World Magazine
Ashville, North Carolina

J. I. Packer
Professor Emeritus
Regent College
Vancouver, Canada

Dorothy Patterson
Professor of Women's
Ministry
Southwestern Baptist
Theological Seminary
Fort Worth, Texas

Paige Patterson
President
Southwestern Baptist
Theological Seminary
Fort Worth, Texas

John Piper
Pastor
Bethlehem Baptist Church
Minneapolis, Minnesota

Vern Poythress
Professor
Westminster Theological
Seminary
Philadelphia, Pennsylvania

Dennis Rainey
President
FamilyLife
Little Rock, Arkansas

W. Duncan Rankin
Professor
Reformed Theological
Seminary
Oak Ridge, Tennessee

Bob Reccord
President
North American Mission
Board (SBC)
Alpharetta, Georgia

Adrian Rogers
Pastor Emeritus
Bellevue Baptist Church
Memphis, Tennessee

Charles Ryrie
Professor Emeritus
Dallas Theological Seminary
Dallas, Texas

R. C. Sproul
Founder & Chairman
Ligonier Ministries
Orlando, Florida

Randy Stinson
Executive Director
The Council on Biblical
Manhood & Womanhood
Louisville, KY

Del Tackett
Executive Vice President
Focus on the Family
Colorado Springs, Colorado

Derek Thomas
Professor
Reformed Theological
Seminary
Jackson, Mississippi

Bruce Ware
Senior Associate Dean of
Theology
The Southern Baptist
Theological Seminary
Louisville, Kentucky

Stu Weber
Pastor
Good Shepherd Community
Church
Boring, Oregon

William C. Weinrich
Academic Dean
Concordia Theological
Seminary
Fort Wayne, Indiana

B. Statement of Concern by Evangelical Scholars

In light of troubling translation inaccuracies - primarily (but not exclusively) in relation to gender language - that introduce distortions of the meanings that were conveyed better by the original NIV, we cannot endorse the 2005 TNIV translation as sufficiently accurate to commend to the church.

Daniel L. Akin, Ph.D.
President
Southeastern Baptist
Theological Seminary

David Allen, Ph.D.
(Linguistics/Homiletics)
Dean
Southwestern Baptist
Theological Seminary

Gregg Allison, Ph.D.
(Systematic Theology)
Professor
The Southern Baptist
Theological Seminary

William Barcley, Ph.D. (New Testament)
Professor
Reformed Theological
Seminary

S. M. Baugh, Ph.D. (New Testament)
Professor
Westminster Theological
Seminary

T. J. Betts, Ph.D.
(Old Testament)
Professor
The Southern Baptist
Theological Seminary

Todd Beall, Ph.D. (Old Testament/New Testament)
Professor
Capital Bible Seminary

David R. Beck, Ph.D.
(New Testament)
Associate Dean
Southeastern Baptist
Theological Seminary

Douglas Blount, Ph.D.
(Philosophy)
Professor
Southwestern Baptist
Theological Seminary

James A. Borland, Th.D.
(Theology)
Professor
Liberty University

Chad Brand, Ph.D.
(Systematic Theology)
Professor
The Southern Baptist
Theological Seminary

Harold O. J. Brown, Ph.D.
Professor
Reformed Theological
Seminary

Robert Cara, Ph.D.
(New Testament)
Professor
Reformed Theological
Seminary

Fred Chay, Ph.D. (Theology)
Professor
Phoenix Seminary

Ray Clendenen, Ph.D.
(Linguistics/Old Testament)
Editor, Broadman & Holman
Nashville, Tennessee

Robert Cole, Ph.D. (Old
Testament/Semitic Lan-
guages)
Professor
Southeastern Baptist
Theological Seminary

Jack Cottrell, Ph.D.
(Theology)
Professor
Cincinnati Bible College and
Seminary

John D. Currid, Ph.D.
(Ancient Near Eastern Lan-
guages and Literature)
Professor
Reformed Theological
Seminary

Dan Doriani, Ph.D.
(New Testament)
Senior Pastor of Central Pres-
byterian Church &
Professor of New Testament
Covenant Theological
Seminary
St. Louis, MO

Iain Duguid, Ph.D.
(Old Testament)
Professor
Westminster Theological
Seminary

Ligon Duncan, Ph.D.
(Theology)
Moderator of PCA; Chairman
of CBMW Board
First Presbyterian Church
Jackson, MS

James V. Fesko, Ph.D.
(Theology)
Professor
Reformed Theological
Seminary

John Frame, D.D.
(Philosophical Theology)
Professor
Reformed Theological
Seminary

Russell Fuller, Ph.D.
(Old Testament)
Professor
The Southern Baptist
Theological Seminary

Paul Gardner, Ph.D.
(New Testament)
Christ Church Presbyterian
Atlanta, GA

Wayne Grudem, Ph.D.
(New Testament)
Professor
Phoenix Seminary

James Hamilton, Ph.D.
(New Testament)
Professor
Southwestern Baptist
Theological Seminary

Daniel Heimbach, Ph.D.
(Christian Ethics)
Professor
Southeastern Baptist
Theological Seminary

Charles E. Hill, Ph.D. (New
Testament/Early Christianity)
Professor
Reformed Theological
Seminary

H. Wayne House, Th.D.
Professor
Faith Seminary
Tacoma, WA

James B. Hurley, Ph.D.
(New Testament)
Professor
Reformed Theological
Seminary

Elliot Johnson, Th.D.
Professor
Dallas Theological Seminary

Jerry Johnson, Ph.D. (Christian Ethics)
Professor
Criswell College

Peter Jones, Ph.D.
(New Testament)
Professor
Westminster Theological
Seminary

David Jussely, Ph.D. (Speech
Communication)
Professor
Reformed Theological
Seminary

R.T. Kendall, Ph.D.
(Philosophy)
Author/Speaker
R.T. Kendall Ministries

George Knight, III, Th.D.
(Theology)
Professor
Greenville Presbyterian
Theological Seminary

Michael J. Kruger, Ph.D.
(New Testament)
Professor
Reformed Theological
Seminary

J. Carl Laney, Th.D.
(Bible Exposition)
Professor
Western Seminary

Richard Mayhue, Th.D.
(Theology)
Dean, School of Theology
Masters Seminary

Eugene H. Merrill, Ph.D.
(Old Testament/Ancient Near
Eastern Studies)
Professor
Dallas Theological Seminary

Eric Mitchell, Ph.D. (Old
Testament)
Professor
Southwestern Baptist
Theological Seminary

R. Albert Mohler, Jr., Ph.D.
(Systematic and Historical
Theology)
President
The Southern Baptist
Theological Seminary

John Moldovan, Ph.D.
Professor
Southwestern Baptist
Theological Seminary

Russell D. Moore, Ph.D.
(Theology)
Dean, School of Theology
The Southern Baptist
Theological Seminary

David Nelson, Ph.D.
Professor
Southeastern Baptist
Theological Seminary

Stan Norman, Ph.D.
(Theology)
Professor
New Orleans Baptist
Theological Seminary

K. Scott Oliphint, Ph.D.
(Historical and Theological
Studies)
Professor
Westminster Theological
Seminary

Raymond C. Ortlund, Ph.D.
(Old Testament)
Senior Pastor
Christ Presbyterian Church
Nashville, Tennessee

James I. Packer, Ph.D.
(Theology)
Professor Emeritus
Regent College

Dorothy Patterson, D.Theol.
(Theology)
Professor
Southwestern Baptist
Theological Seminary

Paige Patterson, Ph.D.
(Theology)
President
Southwestern Baptist
Theological Seminary

John Piper, D.Theol. (New
Testament)
Senior Pastor; Author/
Speaker
Bethlehem Baptist Church

Vern Poythress, Th.D. (New
Testament)
Professor
Westminster Theological
Seminary

Walt Russell, Ph.D. (Herme-
neutics/New Testament)
Professor
Talbot School of Theology

Charles Ryrie, Th.D.
(Systematic Theology)
Professor Emeritus
Dallas Theological Seminary
Dallas, Texas
Editor, *Ryrie Study Bible*

Robert Saucy, Ph.D.
(Systematic Theology)
Professor
Talbot School of Theology

Peter Schemm, Ph.D.
(Theology)
Professor
Southeastern Baptist
Theological Seminary

R.C. Sproul, Ph.D.
Author/Speaker
Ligonier Ministries

Randy Stinson, Ph.D.
(Theology)
Executive Director
The Council on Biblical
Manhood and Womanhood

Sam Storms, Ph.D.
(Theology)
President
Enjoying God Ministries

David Talley, Ph.D.
(Old Testament)
Professor
Talbot School of Theology

Erik Thoennes, Ph.D.
(Theology)
Professor
Talbot School of Theology

Carl Trueman, Ph.D.
(Church History/Historical
Theology)
Professor
Westminster Theological
Seminary

Cornelis P. Venema, Ph.D.
President
Mid-America Reformed
Seminary

Guy Waters, Ph.D.
(New Testament)
Professor
Belhaven College

Bruce Ware, Ph.D.
(Theology)
Associate Dean
Southern Baptist Theological
Seminary

Kevin Warstler, Ph.D.
(Old Testament)
Professor
Criswell College

William C. Weinrich, Ph.D.
(Church History)
Professor
Concordia Theological
Seminary

Gordon Wenham, Ph.D.
(Old Testament)
Professor
University of Gloucestershire

Robert Lee Williams, Ph.D.
Professor
Southwestern Baptist
Theological Seminary

Malcolm Yarnell, *Ph.D.*
(Philosophy)
Professor
Southwestern Baptist
Theological Seminary

For further reading, see:

Journal for Biblical Manhood and Womanhood. 7, no. 2 (Fall 2002) [Special Focus on the TNIV].

Leland Ryken, *The Word of God in English* (Wheaton: Crossway, 2004).

Vern Poythress and Wayne Grudem, *The TNIV and the Gender-Neutral Bible Controversy* (Nashville: Broadman and Holman, 2004).

www.no-tniv.com

To obtain more copies of this publication, contact:

The Council on Biblical Manhood and Womanhood
(CBMW)
2825 Lexington Road, Box 926
Louisville, KY 40280
888.560.8210
office@cbmw.org
www.cbmw.org